Rooted in His love

My Identity is God's love for Me

Debbie Jones

Cover design and layout by Debbie Jones

Photography, logo, and graphics by Brian Jones — BRJDesigns.com

GraceAnthems.com

To order additional copies of this resource go to the website or write to:

Debbie.GraceAnthems@gmail.com

Grace ANTHEMS

Table of Contents

Dedication

This book is lovingly dedicated to my Heavenly Father, for **TOTALLY** loving me with His True Love. He has completely captivated my heart and my greatest desire is to honor Him. All the good fruit that springs forth from me is by the empowering of the Holy Spirit, by God's amazing grace.

Acknowledgments

I want to thank my husband, Gary, for believing in me to get this book published. Our son Brian for his incredible artistic talent and support as we designed this cover and also the logo and graphics. Our two daughters, Jennifer and Andrea for their perspective on design and editing. Our three dogs, Bailey, Bentley, and Diamond for their minimal barking so I could concentrate. My friends, you know who you are, you have been like Moses' friends to me, helping me to hold up my arms to God in ceaseless praise as I forged ahead in the battle. Jack Begley who asked me to write this study for a support group curriculum and gave me a deadline to get it done. And finally, Dave Anorve who spent hours helping me with my computer and scanning the original back in when my hard drive crashed. This book has been a work of love and perseverance!

About the Author

One of Debbie Jones' passions is bringing the Word of God to life. With the firm belief that each one of us has a unique destiny and that it is fulfilled best within the bounty of a deep loving relationship with God, the Lord has set her heart ablaze as a catalyst to boldly proclaim that you can do anything in life if you know you are totally loved. Knowing for certain that many people struggle with a sense of their worth and purpose, she has felt a strong call to help shepherd, guide and lead people into freedom as they discover who they are in Him.

Sensing this strong call from the Lord, along with a desire to live out the dreams that seemed to keep nagging away at her, she felt a bit disillusioned until God revealed to her that she had, in many ways, been possessing and living out this dream and call already. She discovered what it means to minister to the heart of God and has been enjoying Him with a new zeal ever since. The Lord confirmed to her that as she ministers to Him, ministry to people would flow forth from there, and it has. All around her while she was mostly unaware, many people through her walk with God have seen, witnessed and discovered for themselves how to be captivated by Him. Through transparency and vulnerability, she has chosen to be real.

Debbie is a lover of people and is constantly inspired to bring about connection and community. She also craves being in nature and loves to spend time walking in the park (or forest) with friends and or the Lord. Music and beauty light her heart on fire, and she is a tenacious worshiper with a constant longing to give honor to the King.

Debbie was born in Redwood City California, moved to New Jersey at the age of 9 months and returned to California when she was 12. After touring across the country and stepping foot over her lifetime in almost every state in America, she now lives in Mesa Arizona with her husband, Gary. This past year they celebrated 31 years of marriage. They have three grown children: Jennifer, Brian, and Andrea.

Endorsements

Over the years I've known Debbie as a passionate lover of God. She gives her total commitment in everything she does and her teaching is of the highest quality. I know you will be blessed and inspired as you learn to grow in your pursuit and love for God.

♦ **Gerry Kinley**

This study was my second with Debbie. She is an excellent teacher with a true heart for God. As a new Christian, Debbie was very patient and thoroughly explained all of my questions. This study is a must for all Christians to truly understand the meaning of covenant.

♦ **Tracy Lorance**

There are not enough beautiful adjectives to describe my wonderful friend and mentor, Debbie Jones. So let me take a few moments to endeavor to do so. If I had to sum her up in just one sentence, It would be: Debbie is the personification of the constantly flowing, living, breathing heart of God bursting forth from a beloved daughter with such overwhelming fullness that it floods His tangible love and presence over all other creations in its path.

Debbie's enthusiasm for pursuing and loving God with a passion is infectious. She is truly rooted and grounded in God's love. More importantly, it is so astoundingly obvious that this is a twofold relationship between herself and the great I AM, that it inspires others to want the same incredible level of God's love in their own lives. I know this for a fact because I am one of those inspired individuals myself. I have taken this Bible study under Debbie and can attest to its life-changing revelation into God's heart for His children.

If you embrace this study with all your heart, God will embrace you back with all of His; for in it, you will learn why your true identity is God's overwhelming love for you. Nothing else (either externally or internally) can ever label you anything less than God's beloved child in whom He is well pleased.

♦ **Brenda Steigerwalt**

The easiest way for me to describe Debbie Jones to others is to refer to Martha's sister Mary in the Bible. Debbie has a heart of worship for God and a desire to be in His presence like no one else I've ever met. This lady walks the walk. Her passion for Jesus and His love emanates from every cell of her being. Her deepest desire is to share that passion and His love with others. She is a gifted teacher, speaker, and pastor. I'm honored to call her friend.

♦ **Terri Petersen**

'Rooted In His Love' by Debbie Jones included "ah ha" moments and was a turning point in my understanding of how deep God's love is for me. It was then that my personal relationship with God grew in maturity. God has gifted Debbie to put into words the meaning of covenant, especially the covenant between God and His people. This 7 week study will leave a lasting impact on anyone who journeys through it.

♦ **Shawntel Roberts**

I am blessed to have been in several of Debbie Jones' Bible studies. Her passion and deep love for our Lord and Savior shines brightly when she's sharing all that God continues to reveal to her and also through the teaching of others about Him! God has been nudging her for years to write Bible studies and to share all that God, through the Holy Spirit, is teaching her about who He is!

It is so obvious spending time with her that her heart overflows with the Lord's love and desire for us to know Him better! Her knowledge of the scriptures enables her to cross reference scripture verses and to explain the Bible in better detail. I have learned so much by her teaching and trust that God is going to continue revealing more amazing things in her calling as a Pastor and teacher of God's Word.

♦ **Susan Gilbert**

All the years I've known Debbie, she has truly inspired me in dynamic ways. She took the time to guide me and we have had many hours of praying together. In return, this has been life-changing for me through my trials and tragedies. Most of all, this has taught me to go to a much deeper level with Jesus; to be the true lover of my soul!

♦ **Kristi Bray**

Debbie has a great love, heart, and passion for the Father, Son and the Holy Spirit. She is a wonderful teacher, she is authentic and true in her writings by sharing her real life experiences which have given me hunger for more knowledge. Debbie introduced to and led me to a deeper understanding of the Holy Spirt. Her compassion and spirit have helped me get closer to God. Debbie has inspired me with my walk with God.

♦ **Christine Ferreira**

Introduction

There has been a driving force inside of me to get this incredible message of God's love through covenant, out for all the world to see. I know that it has been written down before, in fact, it is written about in the most perfect book of all, the Bible. So, why do I have this compelling need to add to the teachings that are already out there? Because it changed my life! And I hope that I will convey it clearly enough to you that it will help change your life as well. Understanding covenant freed me to trust in the security of God's love and promises while living in and through life's circumstances. You know the kind, they mess with your whole sense of identity and self-worth. They keep you tossing and turning during the night. And one of our greatest human needs is to feel secure and loved. But often we feel anxious, scared and even lonely and rejected. Our minds churn with apprehensions. We have waves of fear, memories of put-downs and brush-offs, and thoughts of people we have to answer to or please. It seems we spend our lives looking for relief. Most of us look for it 'in all the wrong places'; I know I do at times. Putting ourselves in the right position and knowing it for certain, can give us answers that affect every part of our lives.

I am hoping to open up the mystery to what may have been hidden or blurred from your view, and quite frankly not talked about that often in or around the church. Understanding the details of God's perfect plan, sometimes painted through symbolism, says more than words can ever say! A strength of trust and security forms deep inside of your soul when you realize the powerful reality of God's covenant love, maybe even repairing, reshaping and enhancing your whole understanding of Him. Everything God does is because of covenant. I pray that a new awareness of what it means to be a friend of God will emerge and bring forth an assurance that can never be taken away from you. To embrace this covenant is to know and feel that Someone **TOTALLY** loves you and believe HIM.

Below is our theme scripture passage

"I pray that out of his glorious riches he may strengthen you with power through faith. And I pray that you, being rooted and established in love, may have power, together with all the saints, to grasp how wide and long and high and deep is the love of Christ, and to know this love that surpasses knowledge – that you may be filled to the measure of all the fullness of God.

Now to him who is able to do immeasurably more than all we ask or imagine, according to his power that is at work within us, to him be glory in the church and in Christ Jesus throughout all generations, forever and ever! Amen." Ephesians 3:16-21.

One of my burning desires is to have a passion for the Lord. He showed me that if I truly want this.........then I must study hard Jesus's passion for me! In other words, I must study hard Jesus's love for me. I've just got to know that somebody TOTALLY loves me and live my life confident in the reality of this fact. I learned that our relationships with other people stem from how genuinely we comprehend that we are in THIS love. It actually makes all of the difference in the world. I hope that I have at least peeked your curiosity? I know I am not alone in my desire to find out if there is something more in life than what I have already known and believed. When you have the knowledge of your real identity, the struggle to feel whole and content will no longer consume your daily life. You can live out of the fullness of God's beautiful True Love when you become firmly convinced that God's covenant is powerful and sacred.

This life enriching revelation can be approached in different ways such as a book, a devotional or through journaling. But, I chose to put this in Bible Study form. Not necessarily to have it be 'A' Bible Study but to give you the opportunity of mining out the nuggets along with me, one piece or perhaps chunk at a time. This method had a much greater impact on my soul then just reading about it. Because of this, as the Lord revealed Himself to me, it sank deeper and rooted and established more noticeably into my whole being.

Welcome!

I am so excited you are joining in with me on this dramatic and stirring journey! I am convinced that as the Spirit of God moves, He can transform your heart to see things a little differently than before you opened the pages of this study. Yes, I am eager for you to discover the treasures that are beckoning from the heart of God. The exquisite detail that He presents throughout scripture is unequaled. He has forever taken my breath away because God is altogether astonishing! Oh that your heart would root so deeply into Him that you can think of nothing else but Him and that He becomes your greatest delight.

Get ready; this is going to be a remarkable adventure!

In preparing this study, I chose to use the New International Version of the Bible. As you answer the questions, they flow into the blanks and boxes best with this translation. Each week is divided into five sections. They can be done daily for five days or all at one sitting because they continue one section to the next as a unit. I also realize that understanding this topic is needed whether you are male or female, so it is not gender bias.

I included a Personal / Leader Guide at the back of this book. You may want to read through it before you start the first week. Some of the topics include worship, prayer and forming a group.

I am narrating this book through the eyes of the energy and power this has had on my own life. I know from reading other people's books and listening to teachings that it is important and helpful to be a part of some-one else's story. Therefore, I chose to open myself up and share from the deepest places at the center of who I am. The italicized sections throughout this study are my personal story. Thank you in advance for the great honor of walking with you as you glean what the Lord is enthusiastic to reveal to you. In the end, you will have YOUR OWN story!

Week 1
Covenant's Impact

This week

I know we all want to start at the impactful mesmerizing parts, to go for it and jump right in. I agree. So we will begin with the solid, irrefutable nuts and bolts of our study—defining what covenant actually is and the steps to enter into this bond. This may sound a little tedious, but I assure you it's enriching. Go ahead and put your faith out there as this is a catalyst to thrust you up and over the threshold into a new forward motion. Forming a good foundation is important. We tend to skip past the core strengthening wisdom. I believe that this is one of the enormous reasons we don't unquestionably grasp the intense love of the Father. I think that you will find this to be fascinating. After we establish the meaning and the process, we will continue in our study this week, by looking at covenant from a human perspective, starting first from this angle because it is a closer match to our natural understanding. As we identify with the heartfelt commitment, substance, and feelings of what it is like for two people, David and Jonathan, to enter into an everlasting pact, we can begin to grasp the ardent weightiness of our covenant with God.

Getting Ready:

Each week will contain this 'Getting Ready' section. It is included so that you can let your heart and mind move into and upon God and His Word. As we begin each week, you will find that it is essential to pray and ask the Holy Spirit to illuminate His Word to you and to let Him bring clarity and insight to what you will study. Without Him, you are just going through an academic lesson with little power to effect any regeneration. Enjoy God! Marvel at HIM!! He so longs for you to be thrilled with His unfailing eternal covenant.

As you prepare to delve into this study today, it is important to note that the Bible is divided into two Testaments that are linked together because they both tell one story. What we refer to as the Old Testament says what is going to happen and the New Testament tells what did happen. It is all about the beautiful love story of God entering into a blood covenant with man through the Lord Jesus Christ.

The most serious, sacred, and secure of all bonds is the blood covenant involving two people. Its value is the closest, and the most enduring of promises. Without question, it can never be broken or altered because you are permanently pledging your life, unconditional love, and protection to the other forever for the walk and the journey.

What is the root meaning behind the blood covenant? The two covenant individuals enter into such a devoted and intimate relationship with one another that **everything** they are and possess is offered without hesitation at any moment because of True Love.

First

I would like to start with just a bit of my story.

The feelings of gut-wrenching rejection plagued me most of my life. I didn't realize the crazy effect this was having on me and the truly desperate need I had to be cut loose. It turned out to be painful, agonizing and, a slow drawn out process. But, when you are set free you are never the same. Looking back now, I can tell you it was worth it all. When I do look back, I can see that I knew I had an undercurrent brewing. I just didn't want to admit that it was as big of a problem as it was and how the darkness I felt was just hovering over me. I had experienced devastating wounds that permeated every crevice of my soul. If these deep hurts were not healed in me, there would continue to be a constant reoccurring plague of anguish and torment. God has been completely faithful to show me the way out. He has overwhelmed me with His touch, and there is now a definite knowing in my core of His True Love. Restoration has been both from His beautiful grace and also from my diligence to persevere. I would like to add, that it was frustrating at times and I did have many instances I felt derailed and sidetracked. However, there was always something inside of me that couldn't give up.

What I discovered permanently changed me. The key to this transformation, out from under rejections rapids, centers on embracing and being fully rooted in God's love. I found out that I can 'know' the love of Christ. There is this place, this amazing place that we can enter into and understand. A spot in His love.

Inside of me is an intense longing for you to accept and experience the profound healing love of God. No matter what you struggle with, even in the hidden spaces and spots others and even you, don't fully comprehend, there can be freedom, and security. My sincere desire is that you encounter the Living Lord. It may begin for you at a crossroad—a place of discovery. Will you step forward and tenaciously keep seeking to find this change in your life?

I believe you want this. So, the first thing we are going to do is get acquainted with how one enters into a sacred bond or pact. In the section above we received a concise definition, and we will be reviewing it each week. What do we really mean by a covenant? This term is universally used in our world and is found in every culture that has ever been discovered. It has lost most of its significance in today's society, especially here in America. What the blood covenant meant to the earliest of people, it still means today. The problem is we have failed to understand its true meaning.

To fully appreciate covenant we will spend some time getting to know the steps and terminology so that we will be able to clearly identify it when we come upon it in the Bible.

Please read each step: (It may be helpful to visualize this in your mind.) * Taken from—The Steps In Making A Blood Covenant Presentation, http://www.rockofoffence.com/myst4.html

1. An animal is sacrificed:

Usually, a bull, a goat, or a lamb is killed and cut in half down the center. The two halves separated by a pool of blood between them.

2. The exchange of coats:

Each participant removes his coat, a sign of their tribe's identity and authority, and gives it to the other participant. By doing so, each is saying, "Everything I am, everything I represent now belongs to you."

3. The exchange of weapon belts:

Each participant removes his weapon belt, which includes his sword and bow. They would exchange these belts and, by so doing, declare to each other, "All my strength now belongs to you. My enemies are now your enemies." It was stating that when an enemy attacked, then my blood covenant brother had a responsibility to defend me the same as he would himself.

4. The exchange of names:

Each participant takes the other's name. A person's name represents his individuality. This exchange of names demonstrated a death to being an individual. Remember that covenant is the union of two people. In covenant you are no longer concerned only with yourself. Your concern now includes your blood covenant partner. You care for your blood brother the same as you care for yourself because the two of you are now one.

5. The walk of blood:

Each participant walks a path in the shape of a figure "8" between the halves of the slain animal. They stop in the middle in the midst of the pool of blood to pronounce the blessings and the curses of the covenant. The curses would be brought to bear upon the one who broke the blood covenant. A pledge was also made that said, "Just as this animal gave its life, so I will give my life for you".

6. The making of the scar:

A knife is used to make an incision in the wrists of each participant. This was to allow blood to flow freely. The Bible teaches that life is in the blood. The two participants engage in a handshake allowing the blood to intermingle. This symbolized the two bloods, the two lives, being joined into one blood and one life. As they heal a permanent mark or scar would be left. Wherever they went they would be identified as being in covenant by the visible marks on their bodies. From now on they would be known as friends! And, all of their children are included in it, even the unborn ones. However, each descendent must choose to be in this covenant for themselves.

7. The covenant meal:

This is usually a meal of bread and wine. Each fed the other signifying that, "all that I am is coming into you." The covenant meal usually ended the blood covenant ceremony. At this point, a new relationship is born. It is a love relationship. This kind of love is called Hesed in Hebrew and Agape in the Greek. It is a love that says, "I will never leave you or forsake you."

Please review each of these steps this week and write out each step below:

1. An animal is sacrificed
2. The exchange of coats
3. _____
4. _____
5. _____
6. _____
7. _____

From Step 6 please answer the following questions:

What are the two covenant partners known as after they cut covenant?_____

Who is included in their covenant?_____

What do these descendants have to do to be in covenant?_____

From these seven steps, what were some of the most significant things you learned?

_____

_____

What are some of the symbolisms you saw between this ritual and your life in Christ (If you are a Christian.)? (Example: exchanging names - we take the name of our covenant partner we are a 'Christ'ian)

_____

_____

Now, any time you see these steps or these words referenced in the Bible, either actually or symbolically, you know that the two are entering into a blood covenant. They may not be spelled out step by step because during the Bible times everyone knew about covenant. This friendship is entirely different. We don't really know much about this type of friendship. Every day we enter into relationships with people with no deep connections, ties or bonds and we don't even intend to be absolutely faithful to them, especially for life. This depth of friendship is so foreign that we have a hard time comprehending it exists.

Marriage can be a covenant union. Marriage is distinctive and is sometimes considered a covenant if taken with these serious requirements.

Second

I want to keep developing this concept of friendship by studying the example of David and Jonathan's covenant. For anyone not familiar with their endearing story we will begin with Samuel the Prophet. The Nation of Israel wanted a king. All the other nations appeared to be reveling in this type of rule. They seemed not to be satisfied with the Lord as their King. So, God honored their desire and gave Samuel the task of declaring His appointed choice for the first king over Israel. Saul was chosen.

The king of Israel was subject to the law of the Lord and the word of the prophets. He was an instrument of the Lord's rule over the people. Over time King Saul demonstrated that he was unwilling to submit to the requirements of his office. When Saul chose not to completely fulfill what the Lord had instructed him to do he was rejected by God as king, and the Spirit of the Lord left him. (He did remain as king, but the Spirit of God was no longer present over his life.) David was anointed as the Lord's choice to be Saul's successor. David waited for a long time as many years passed before he took the throne.

David, the youngest son of Jesse, was a shepherd. Described as a handsome and brave warrior and a devout worshiper of the Lord. He was known for playing the harp and being a man after God's own heart. The key aspect of his life was that the Lord was with David (see - 1Sam 16:18). David refused to usurp Saul's throne even though he knew God had anointed him to be king. He waited on God's perfect timing with no attempts to use any worldly means of force. David had numerous opportunities to take Saul's life. One was inside of a cave while Saul was sleeping. David could easily have had one of his guards kill Saul, but David chose to have a piece of Saul's robe cut off instead.

Saul was extremely jealous of David, and he tried to have him killed on numerous occasions. Eventually, Saul was wounded in battle, and he took his own life. Saul was the father of three sons. One of which was David's loyal friend Jonathan who was also killed in that battle. Jonathan had loved David and became one with him in spirit through covenant. Jonathan had protected David from the wrath of his father, risking his life.

After highlighting a few key components of Jonathan and David's relationship, we will now look at specific parts of their covenant in greater detail.

Please read 1 Samuel 18:1-4:

What covenant terminology do you see here? Which of the 7 steps we have just studied were mentioned in this passage?

_____

Please read 1 Samuel 20:13-17, 23, 41&42:

List some of the covenant steps as you consider how all these verses are part of their covenant?

_____

God seemed to knit their hearts together.

This relationship was one of the most sincere friendships described in the Bible. It is the clearest Old Testament picture of the covenant relationship that we have with Christ.

There are some characteristics of this covenant relationship which can be a model for strong, healthy friend-ships today. One particular aspect would be the incredible idea that they became one in spirit. It's not often that God just knits two hearts together. If a person has one relationship in life like this, then he or she is fortunate.

God gave me a friend like this many years ago. Our sons were friends and in the same grade at school. Our families would go camping and skiing together, sharing, laughing and enjoying good times. I also had the privilege of leading her to the Lord one evening, in my husband's convertible, under the stars. She and I would go for walks and spend time praying together. We related well with each other providing inspiration that helped each of us heal from past hurts. There was something special between us that only the Lord could have woven together, I just loved her with the love of the Lord. Then we moved away from each other. At first, we would still plan trips to do things together, but as time went by, unfortunately, something reached in and stole what we had developed. She distanced herself from me to the point of no contact and, it hurts to say this, but I really don't know why. In fact, I felt betrayed. Healing took a long time, and I'm not sure I will ever be completely free from the scar on my heart. Even though we aren't in communication with each other, there is a bond of love I have for her that will be with me permanently. I've never gotten over the impact she has had on my life, the covenant impact.

Please jump ahead with me in our story to 2 Samuel 1:25-26:

Jonathan has died, and David is mourning his death. Do you sense the deep love of covenant friendship they shared toward each other?_____

Please read 2 Samuel 4:4: What events took place?

_____

_____

After Saul and Jonathan's death, we see that the nurse fled, carrying Jonathan's five-year-old son, Mephibosheth. She was fleeing because she feared David would come to harm them since there appeared to be no further protection from Saul's reign. She believed the lie assuming David hated Saul and therefore Saul's family too. The only harm that came was to Mephibosheth's feet; they were crippled when the nurse dropped him in her haste. If Saul's household had known the love that Jonathan and David shared, they wouldn't have fled, and no injury would have occurred. As Mephibosheth grew up, he blamed and feared David and hardened his heart to him.

Below describe how you can relate to either of these two types of situations (my story or that of Mephibosheth):

_____

_____

_____

Third

We wrap up our research in the Bible this week by continuing briefly in the book of Samuel.

Please read 2 Samuel 9:1-13:

David was faithful to God and therefore to any covenant agreement he had sworn in the sight of his Lord. He did not forget his promise to Jonathan. What does David ask the servant in Saul's household? Please examine the scriptures below.

Read 2 Samuel 9:1 below:

"David asked, "Is there anyone still left of the house of Saul to whom I can show kindness for Jonathan's sake?"

Read 2 Samuel 9:3 below:

"The king asked, "Is there no one still left of the house of Saul to whom I can show God's kindness?"

Whose kindness did David want to show, Jonathan's, or did he have Someone else's in mind? Whose kindness did he really want to show? _____

Who did David initiate a search for in **verses 3 & 4**? _____

What was the name of the place they found him in **verse 5**? _____

What was Mephibosheth's response in **verse 6**? _____

David could sense that he was afraid. What was David's reason for being kind?

_____

What was David going to do for Mephibosheth?

_____

_____

What was Mephibosheth's response and what did he say in **verse 8**?

_____

I am sure that Mephibosheth couldn't believe his ears! This is the king who hated him, or so he thought, the one who he had in turn feared and run from because of a misunderstanding. He may have even said horrible things about him, making jokes, voicing insults and turning away from him his whole life. Suddenly he realized that there had been a mistake. There was nothing he could do to earn anything back or make up for all the misinterpretations. But the error and misjudgments would soon be clearly understood as he found out that

David had a different heart. One of compassion and kindness. A heart in covenant.

Because of the covenant of love David had for Mephibosheth's father Jonathan, he followed through with his promise to restore back the land belonging to his grandfather, Saul. He had servants assigned to farm the land and bring in the crops. Sounds like a wonderful new life! What an incredible blessing for Mephibosheth.

Where do you see Mephibosheth dining in 2 Samuel 9:11?

_____

Who is he like?_____

Please keep this last phrase tucked closely in your heart - **'Like one of the king's sons'.**

Fourth

We can see how David honored his covenant with Jonathan. Please note the covenant symbolism.

Mephibosheth's story (a picture or portrait) of God's covenant with us can become like a precious gem or a crown jewel to you as you see the far-reaching effects of the solemn, binding agreement of covenant. David took the initiative and fulfilled his covenant commitment. If a human can act with such faithfulness, even under those difficult circumstances, the realization can begin to evolve of just how much more we can trust our Covenant God to fulfill His 'Covenant Agreement'. He has said to us, "All that I possess is now yours. All of My power belongs to you." We have an incredible inheritance because of the covenant that Christ made with us. One of our personal reminders of this is experienced in The Lord's Supper. Every time we participate in this great symbolic moment, we can consider and are encouraged to remember, the covenant that we have with Him. We have entered into the deepest of relationships known to man.

This story is more than just words or events that took place. Let it get into your heart. The symbolism helps us understand that God's covenant with us is personal yet far-reaching. The covenant was not only between the two men, David and Jonathan but also with each of their descendants. Mephibosheth was one of those descendants. (In God's covenant we are a descendant of Abraham. We will learn this next week.)

Mephibosheth appeared to know nothing of the covenant. All his years he thought David was out to kill him. He was aware that David was king, the ultimate authority and power of the nation, but he didn't 'know' David. All he knew was what others had told him. He didn't understand this king's, heart. What a difference it would have made. He fled for no reason. All those years of running and hating had been building up inside of Mephibosheth. Now he couldn't believe it! It was inconceivable! You see, he just didn't have the facts straight. He had lived in ignorance of the covenant made by his father. If only he had known, then he could have run to David and claimed his position in the covenant.

He had to make a choice! He had free will. He must either enter into the covenant with David or keep running and hiding in Lo-debar. (The name of the city meant 'no pasture' describing his situation there - barren.)

How was Mephibosheth's choice a difficult one to make? And how is this similar to our choosing to enter into covenant with Jesus Christ?

_____

_____

The man he had hated all of his life he would now choose to love with all of his heart. He would become one with someone he ran from and feared. He must humble himself, admit he was wrong and turn his back on his old ways of thinking about David. What about all of his friends who may have heard him ridicule and make fun of David, what will they think of him in this new role? Not that easy of a choice after all. We all struggle with pride.

What might be some things we are told about God that keep us running from Him?

_____

He spent his life in fear, running and hiding. He now felt unworthy of David's mercy and love. David's KINDNESS!! He had to realize though that the covenant had nothing to do with him. Mephibosheth was just a recipient of the great love his father and David had for one another — a binding covenant. That covenant meant everything to David. In addition to David's love for Jonathan, he also wanted to show God's kindness.

Despite Mephibosheth's unbelief in the beginning, he eventually believed it was true and chose to sit at David's table like one of the king's sons. No one could force him to do this; no one could force the covenant on him. His monumental decision would have long lasting effects; he had to change his thinking on the things he once believed.

Fifth

We have just gotten our feet wet in discovering covenant. Did you go over the seven steps of cutting covenant this week? Even if you haven't this is a good time, as I remind you, to immerse this deep into your heart and mind.

Please don't skip this exciting part. This is where we start to put all the pieces together:

I hope you are beginning to see how the covenant of Jonathan and David is a picture of our relationship with God.

Here are just a few questions for you to ponder. Remember these are all representations and symbols:

Who do you think David represents in this story? (loosely - because of his desire to show kindness) G_____

God wants to take us out of our barren wilderness and adopt us into His own family so we can sit and dine at His table with Him.

Jonathan belongs to what family? S_____

What was Saul's attitude towards God? _____

Did Jonathan act like he belonged in the family of Saul?_____

Who was Jonathan like because of their covenant? D_____

David delighted to do the will of God. If David represents God in this story Who does Jonathan represent (again very loosely)? J_____   C_____

Based on our seven steps from the beginning of this week's study, list some things Jesus has done for you in covenant :

_____
_____
_____
_____

So, maybe you can't or couldn't believe your ears!! Before you were a Christian just like Mephibosheth you may have run from God, even hated Him, maybe you joked about Him. At that point, you didn't yet know His heart. The King who hated you or so you thought. Who you in turn feared and ran from because of misunderstanding. You may have even said horrible things about God, voicing insults and turning away from Him your whole life. Suddenly you realized that there had been a mistake. There was nothing you could do to earn anything or make up for all the misinterpretation. The error and misjudgments were replaced as you found out that the Lord has a different heart. One of compassion and kindness. A heart in covenant.

When we choose to enter into covenant with Jesus Christ, we are accepting God's mercy and love. We are able to see how we have feared and run from God, how we have dreaded what life would be like under His authority. When we finally see what covenant truly means, we will desperately desire to enter into this lasting binding union. We will change our thinking on the things we once believed, God will see to it, as His Spirit lives in us. He will weed out the lies and transform our heart with the truth. No one can force God's covenant on us. We must make a choice to sit at the King's table as a 'son' (or daughter).

The 7 steps we began our study with this week are all fulfilled in Jesus. Please read each one again with Jesus in mind:

Jesus is your covenant partner!

1. Jesus is the Lamb as the sacrifice.
2. He has exchanged robes with you, giving you His white coat of righteousness for your filthy black coat of sin.
3. He is your shield and defender, giving you His strength to fight your battles.
4. He has exchanged names with you.
5. He has given you the Holy Spirit as the seal of your inheritance.
6. He has exchanged natures with you. The symbolic intermingling of His blood that was shed on the cross speaks of you being joined with Him as one, and you now have a new heart.
7. He has also given you all of His assets, treasure and wealth, for all your liabilities. Lock stock and barrel. Amazing!

In closing for this week, let's think together. You are a believer, right? You have asked Jesus to be your substitute, your beloved Savior. (If not then there is a place at the back of this book for you to turn to that explains this in more detail). God has accepted you in the covenant because of Jesus. The Holy Spirit has sealed you and is living in you. Please dig down into the depths of your soul. Jesus stands at the door of your heart. He knows you have entered into covenant with Him.

Read out loud Revelation 3:20 that follows:

"Here I am! I stand at the door and knock. If anyone hears my voice and opens the door, I will come in and eat with him, and he with me."

Remember that Mephibosheth came to eat at the king's table. Remember he was like one of the king's sons.

Are you consciously answering Jesus' knock? To have a relationship with Jesus you have to hear His voice and open the door. He doesn't force Himself on you. He waits for you to open the door. Your covenant partner loves you and loves to spend time with you. For some of us, though, this is a hard reality to grasp, that He desires to dine with us. Yes, it is true He does desire to dine with you! As you get to know the commitment, essence and feelings that the Lord has for you because of His covenant love, your heart is sure to burst forth in joy. **Sometimes it takes knowing the truth to be able to rest fully in its reality.** Sometimes it takes knowing what you have before you truly appreciate it. So at this point in our study, you may not be all that sure yet, and things may not be as deep or intimate as you are longing for, and that is OK. In fact, that is why we are developing a greater awareness of this knowledge. To help you expand, blossom and thrive to the point where your heart will be able to believe this True Love.

Please think about your current understanding of covenant. At this moment can you feel the bond and commitment that David had for Jonathan and subsequently for his son Mephibosheth? Can you place yourself right there at the table as if you were Mephibosheth? Don't you think that it is entirely possible, given

David's heart and all that David had done for Mephibosheth, that eventually Mephibosheth must have established an emotional tie to David.

This is true for you and me as well. Wherever your heart is currently in your personal love for the Lord— this is your side of the covenant. If I may ask, is your side heartfelt?

The Lord is faithful. He is waiting. If you open the door, Jesus promised He would come in and dine with you. When you dine with someone, you get more and more acquainted with them.

You at the King's table!!! Is it drive-through, family-style or candle-light? Why did you give this answer?

Below are some topics you can discuss with the Lord as you dine together:

(These apply even as a believer. Remember it is essential for your thinking to change. The Holy Spirit is your guide and teacher, and He gives you His empowering grace to enable you to believe and to grow.)

1. Am I crippled because I have run from really knowing You God (Your heart)?

2. Am I still dwelling in the poverty of Lo-debar when I could be understanding and enjoying the richness of the inherited covenant?

3. Do I fear that if I come to You God and bow before You and faithfully surrender, that You will do some harm to me? Do I fear the rug being ripped out from under me because I don't really trust the Covenant?

Wait— Stop!! These are lies. You need to know the heart of your King. **HIS KINDNESS!!**

1. God knows you, and He loves you as His son or daughter.

2. The Lord has bestowed upon you an extraordinary heritage.

3. God is always good, and He always has the best for you, His beloved child.

Pull up your special seat at the heavenly table as you dine with your family in the covenant of God.

Next week

We will explore the depth of God's covenant of love and see what we have entered into and what this truly means. As we zoom in to get a clear image, it is sure to give you a new focus.

Week 2

New Lens - Clearer Focus

Last week

We spent time studying the district blood covenant between David and Jonathan that portrays the beautifully painted picture of God's covenant with His people. We saw how this directly affected Mephibosheth's life. Remember with me what we have learned. Because of covenant, Mephibosheth was set apart, but he didn't know it. Before he chose to enter into covenant with David, he was running hard and fast in the opposite direction fearing, blaming and hiding because he didn't have the facts straight. But upon accepting David's request, his whole life changed.

Yours can too! Let's review some of the things that you take hold of in your covenant with God. When King Jesus looks at you, He sees you not as crippled and lame. He sees you from His perspective as one for whom the covenant was cut. God says, "Stop running around in your barren place of Lo-debar. I've searched for you and found you, and have chosen for you to dine with Me." This is exciting! As we keep studying covenant, the eyes of your heart can be enlightened to see just what you truly have in God. I long for you to see the parallels of Mephibosheth's story and have that forever enhance your life.

This week

We are going to set the lens of our heart to see at a more fixed position right into the depth of God's covenant - the Abrahamic Covenant. This journey is rich and stunning. If you are willing, God is waiting expectantly to reveal Himself to you in a close up picture. Set up your tripod and focus the zoom lens and allow it to show an image that is sure to cause you to gaze in wonder.

Getting Ready:

I would like to make a statement here. This is very serious! The covenant of God is so serious; it shouldn't be taken glibly or lightly. Remember that the essence of blood covenant love is loyalty; your God is loyal. Please, before you start digging into scripture, spend some time with the Lord lifting His great and holy name on high. Ask him to show you what you cannot see on your own. God is good, and He wants you to know Him, in and through, His covenant.

The most serious, sacred, and secure of all bonds is the blood covenant involving two people. Its value is the closest, and the most enduring of promises. Without question, it can never be broken or altered because you are permanently pledging your life, unconditional love, and protection to the other forever for the walk and the journey.

First

We begin by meeting another person in the Bible, Abram. Who was Abram? Born in 1948 BC, he was the son of Terah, who was a decedent of Shem, who was a son of Noah. You remember Noah. He built the ark, and he and his family were the only ones saved in the flood. Abram was 58 years old when Noah died. This information is significant because he would have received first-hand knowledge not only about the details of the flood but also about creation since it was passed along verbally at that time.

Terah, Abrams father, was an idol worshiper who lived with his family in Ur of the Chaldeans, a very high level cultural city in its era. Abram did not follow his father's gods. Instead, he believed in the one true God, the God of Noah.

Abram had a wife, and her name was Sarai. She was barren; she had no children.

Please read Genesis 12:1-8:

What did God tell Abram to do in the first part of **verse 1**?

_____

Why do you think he was told to leave his father's household?

_____

Where did God say Abram and a few members of his family were to go?

_____

Abram obeyed. He left his country not even knowing where he was going. Somehow there was something in him that resonated with the Lord because Abram just stepped out believing God would lead him.

How old does it say Abram was in **verse 4**? _____

From the next verses list the promises made to Abram by God:

1. "I will make you a _____ "
2. "I will _____ "
3. "I will make your _____ "
4. "and you will be a _____ "
5. "I will bless those who _____ "
6. "and whoever curses you I will _____ "
7. "all peoples on earth will be blessed _____ "

What was another promise God made to Abram in **verse 7**? _____

What land in **verse 5**? _____

Abram believed God, and he trusted God. He obeyed. What a fantastic relationship. Can you imagine packing up your family and leaving behind your clan, your people, your country, your way of life and setting out to the unknown and in a tent no less? Just go! Such faith!

When was the last time you had to trust God with what we might say is 'blind faith'? Consider this, to trust someone with your future like this you must know enough about them to believe they are trustworthy.

God was calling Abram to His blood covenant of love, but at this point, Abram had no idea what this would entail. He was just told to get out of the pagan land of worldly idols where he had been living. Abram knew enough about God to know that He had spoken to him and given him promises. The promises we looked at earlier included making him into a great nation, he would be blessed, and his name would be made great.

The land of Canaan is the 'Promised Land'. God turned to Abram and told him that his offspring would be given this land.

What was Abram's response to God in verse 7?

_____

May I ask you a question? Have you ever had a response to the Lord like this? In your own life what would be that overwhelming that you would build an altar? We don't think about altars now since Jesus died on the cross setting us free from this formal aspect of altar ritual. But, I believe one of the keys to this kind of response to God is that the Lord 'appeared' to Abram. Could this be what it takes for you? What if the Lord appeared to you too? As we proceed through this study together, I hope to help you see how the Lord appears to us, now, this side of the cross. This is the first of many altars Abram built in places that he had memorable experiences with God.

In my life, I have had some incredibly beautiful and unforgettable experiences and also some circumstances that have rocked my world. A few have broken me so deeply to my core that my only response was to bow down in worship. Yes, worship. The Lord is so faithful and He is always there to comfort, guide and support me. I realize now that God is always good and kind. Through these awful situations, God has steadied me, and been building a foundation in my life to show me His covenant of love. One of these occasions was in a subtle way similar to Abram.

In 2001, right after 911 on September 20th, my husband was laid off from his prestigious, well-paying job in the Silicon Valley of the Bay Area, California. He spent months sending out many resumes, but as he put it, "Always the bridesmaid never the bride". So after a year and a half with no income, we packed up our clan, our family, our belongings, our way of life and set out to the desert to Mesa Arizona, but thankfully not in a tent. Just go! Much faith!

To say I was miserable at first, would be a huge understatement. This is definitely not the Promised Land (have you been here?).... We were without a job or any income for another year and a half. During this time I

I would like to make one last point in this section. After Abram had built the altar, he moved on toward the hills of Bethel and pitched his tent, with Bethel on the west and Ai on the east (Genesis 12:8).

Where is his tent in relationship to Bethel and Ai – **circle the correct answer:**

Next to them   In the middle of them   Far away from them

Bethel means 'House of God' and is a symbol of fellowship with God. Ai means 'ruin' and some have said it is a symbol of the world. So symbolically that would mean that Abram pitched his tent between fellowship with God and fellowship with the world. Whether we see this figuratively or not, the idea of positioning our lives between the Lord and the world is an interesting one. It is all too easy to get our tent located incorrectly. Fortunately Abram didn't just park himself between these two places. He built an altar there and called on the Name of the Lord.

Second

We continue in the story of Abram. He later spent some time in Egypt and gained great wealth and possessions. He and his nephew Lot had to part company because of quarreling between their herdsmen. Abram gave Lot his choice of which direction he wanted to go in and Lot chose the east toward the Jordan and pitched his tent near Sodom. Abram settled and lived in the land of Canaan. The Lord reminded Abram of His promise by having him lift up his eyes and look around at all the land that he could see. This would be the land for all of his offspring. They would be like the dust of the earth. If anyone could count the dust, his offspring could be counted. In other words, they would become too numerous to tally.

God brought Abram to the land of Canaan and approached him in a way that Abram could understand, through blood covenant. Remember everyone back then recognized covenant. In fact, blood covenant started back in the Garden of Eden when Adam and Eve sinned. The Lord clothed them by the shedding of the blood of an animal, their sin covering awaiting the promised Redeemer. It is the same covenant God reconfirmed with Noah, and Noah's first response after being cooped up in the ark was to offer a blood sacrifice to the Lord on an altar.

The Lord declared His redemptive plan through blood covenant. It has been heralded out through all the ages. We now have it written down in the Bible.

In the Old Testament, covenant was revealed most clearly to us through Abram. In fact, this is the reason we are studying this in such extensive detail. Once you comprehend the magnitude of this covenant with Abram you will hopefully see, feel and absorb God's intense True Love.

Now we step forward in the story to read Genesis 15:1-9:

What does the shield in **Genesis 15:1** have to do with God's Covenant? (Remember back to the steps of covenant from last week's lesson.)

_____

_____

> "Do not be afraid, Abram,
> I am your shield,
> your very great reward."
> Genesis 15:1

Abram cried out to God, "O Sovereign LORD." He knew God. He knew Him as his Lord and King. He knew God was in control, but he still had questions.

What does Abram question God about in **verses 2 & 3**?

_____

What was the promise God made to Abram in **verses 4 & 5**?

_____

Why was this such an unbelievable thing to Abram at this point in his life (of old age)?

_____

Who are the offspring now?

_____

Write out verse 6 below:

_____

_____

What was the one thing credited to Abram? _____

Abram believed. What was it he believed – **this must be key!**

In verse 7 God reminded Abram that He called him out of Ur of the Chaldeans (known as Babylonia - which represents the world system, its attitudes, and mentality related to the current age). God would give him the land (Canaan), and he would take possession of it.

What was Abram's problem with this according to verse 8?

_____

He could grasp the promise of a son, but he was skeptical about the promise of the land. So how could he have faith enough to believe God? What guarantee did Abram have from God that this would come to pass? The Lord gave him not only reassurance but His faithful and genuine commitment. He answered Abram, but this reply may surprise you.

Please read Genesis 15:9-10:

Did you see it? God gave His answer in covenant.

Let's unpack the details together:

Let your heart begin to focus in. God's moment to start the whole process of unveiling His incredible love story that led up to Jesus Christ and His redemption for humanity is about to unfold. This is covenant language.

What terminology do you see in verses 9 and 10?

_____

_____

A three-year-old heifer, a goat, a ram, along with a dove, and a young pigeon. Reads more like a shopping list. Abram understood perfectly well what God was asking him to prepare to do.

Cut them in two ... and place each piece opposite the other. Abram was cognizant of exactly what to do with these animals. In keeping with the custom of his day, God was telling him to get a different kind of love contract ready for signing.

Remember in those days, bonds and pacts were made by the sacrificial cutting of animals, with the split carcasses of the animals lying on the ground. Then both parties in the covenant walked through the animal pieces together in a figure 8, repeating the terms.

But there was something that remained unclear and unimaginable, and the big question. How was a merely created person going to enter into covenant with God. He is Almighty, perfect, powerful and wonderful. How did Abram have even one thing that God would need or want from him? It must **NOT** be anything from Abram; it must be **ALL** from God. Remember all Abram did was believe!!

These verses describe the events that impacted all of mankind forever!!

Read Genesis 15:12:

What happened to Abram right smack dab in the middle of covenant 'cutting' with God?

_____

God wanted nothing to get in the way, so we see that Abram got some extra sleep! What accompanied his deep sleep?

_____

In Genesis **verses 13-16** what future events did God tell Abram about while he was sleeping?

_____

_____

_____

_____

The fulfillments of these are:

Strangers in a country not your own (Egypt) - see Gen 46:3-4

Enslaved for 400 years - see Ex 12:40

Abram dies at an old age - see Gen 25:8

This is the best part!!

Please read Genesis 15:17&18:

What amazing thing did Abram have the privilege of witnessing? Someone taking his place. Someone walking where he should have been walking. Who was He? Who stood in for Abram? _____

This may be a hard concept to get a good grasp of, that Jesus would stand in and cut covenant with the Father. Why would He? How did He do this? What power this must take. We just have so many questions in our limited thinking, don't we? The magnitude of the idea and the incredible power and glory of God!

Stunning!

Remember that God had Abram fall into a deep sleep. Somehow he was able to speak to Abram about the future as well as reveal this amazing scene right before Abram's eyes. I'm not sure how he saw what he saw in this sleep state, but it is a wonder that keeps us thinking. Especially if you have ever had an operation and been put under but were not completely out - you're 'there' but not really 'there'. A mystery. The Glory.

What words were used to describe Jesus and the Father?

_____

Read Revelation 1:12-16: What words do you see that are similar to the words in Genesis 15:17&18?

_____

This is a glorious description of Jesus. Note in Revelation that the seven 'lamp-stands' represent the churches. Also note that the high priest would wear a full length robe. Jesus is the final and complete High Priest. Complete Royalty! How are you picturing Him in His robe of righteousness? He is the Beautiful One!

Even though it wasn't Abram personally participating in the 'cutting' of covenant, his representative was there to stand in for him. As a result, just as Mephibosheth was Jonathan's descendent, Abram had descendants or seeds too. Who **ARE** Abram's descendants? (remember Mephiboseth? - he had to choose to accept the covenant)

Galatians 3:29 in the New Covenant says, **"If you belong to Christ, then you are Abraham's seed, and heirs according to the promise."**

Romans 9:8, **"In other words, it is not the natural children who are God's children, but it is the children of the promise who are regarded as Abraham's offspring."**

Not all of Abram's descendants though……

Only those who……..believe!!!!!

Believe what? Believe that Christ the Son of God entered into covenant with God the Father on our behalf. The Father and Jesus – A Smoking Firepot (The Father) and a Blazing Torch (Jesus).

"Therefore, if anyone is in Christ, he is a new creation; the old has gone, the new has come!" 2 Corinthians 5:17

I would like to point out that we are **IN** Jesus as a believer. So as Jesus walked through the pieces, we walked through the pieces with Him. Yes, this applies to you, because, before the foundation of the earth God had foreknowledge. He knows all of the past, present and future. He knew you, loved you and as He walked through those pieces, He knew you were **IN** Him.

All of Abram's unborn seed were 'included' in this covenant. Do you see how **YOU** are included? It's through faith that you are **IN** Christ Jesus.

Review:

All of this has been a lot to assimilate so let's spend a moment assessing what has happened. God promised to be Abram's shield and defender. He promised that his offspring would be too numerous to count and that he would possess the land of Canaan. Abram believed God about the descendants but questioned the Lord on the possession of the land. God gave Abram proof positive that He would forever fulfill His promise by permanently 'cutting' covenant, not with Abram as a mere human with nothing to contribute, but with Jesus as his representative.

God 'cut' covenant with Himself. The Father and Jesus – A Smoking Firepot and a Blazing Torch.

We saw that God caused Abram to fall asleep so he wouldn't try any funny business. But, he was enlightened enough to hear God give future events. Most importantly he was witness to this glorious phenomenon, as the Father and King Jesus passed through between the pieces and changed history forever!!

Third

We will summarize **Chapter 16 of Genesis**. Remember God told Abram he would bear a son of his own body. But, after years and years of frustration with no success, he and Sarai took matters into their own hands because they desperately wanted this son that would be the heir. Sarai encouraged Abram to sleep with her Egyptian maidservant named Hagar so that she would conceive. Sarai thought they could build their family through her. According to that time and custom, a childless wife could call herself a mother by giving her maidservant to her husband as a second wife. Hagar's child would be considered the child of Abram and Sarai. Hagar became pregnant, and Sarai became jealous. Hagar fled into the desert to escape Sarai's mistreatment. But God met Hagar and instructed her to return to Sarai, give birth to her child, and name him Ishmael.

Please read Genesis 17:1-8:

Again God restates the covenant. He was sealing the deal so Abram would fully understand both his small part as well as God's part in their everlasting binding blood covenant.

How old was Abram at that time?_____

The Lord 'appeared' to Abram, and his unabashed response to God's great Majesty was to fall face down.

In Genesis 17:5 God and Abram exchange names. What name did God give to Abram?

_____

God's sacred name in Hebrew is YHWH.

What letter from God's name was added to Abram? _____ God took the H out of His name and gave it to Abram, and his new name became AbraHam.

Remembering last week, what is this step in 'cutting' covenant? _____

Can you figure out what name God bore? _____ (answer below)

From this point on in Scripture, we often hear God refer to Himself as, "The God of Abraham, the God of Isaac and the God of Jacob".

We also receive a new name; we are called a Christian, this means 'little Christ.' Now that you are starting to understand covenant, can you see that this is a matter of **identity**; your oneness and reflection of your Partner? We bear His name. God wants us to see how beautiful we truly are in Him and to reflect the radiant character of Christ. Walking in a manner that exudes such an incredible honor.

Remember that one of the parts of covenant partners was that they became friends. Abraham was known from here on out as 'the friend of God'.

"And the scripture was fulfilled that says, "Abraham believed God, and it was credited to him as righteousness, and he was called God's friend." James 2:23

He had a faithful friend forever and ever. And, you have a faithful Friend forever and ever too. You are a friend of God. Maybe you have sung the song 'I am a friend of God' and never quite grasped what this truly means. Think for a moment of what it requires to be a friend of God. What loving value and worth you are to Jesus Christ. You are in covenant with such a magnificent Friend. And friendship is the commitment of one to another.

Look at Genesis 17:7:

Right there it says that this is an everlasting covenant between Abraham and God and all his descendants after him for generations to come.

Fourth

Have you ever thought of this? A relationship (friendship) is two-sided!! No, I am not trying to point out the obvious. But, I would like for you to go with me on a brief visit to a critical period in my life some years ago, an intersection of profound truth in my relationship with the Lord.

Come with me to Sevens Creek Park in Los Altos California in the spring of 1997 on a warm, bright and sunny day. I had gathered up my Bible, a journal, and pen and driven a few miles from my home. Arriving at the park, I could see that there were no other cars in the parking lot and my heart skipped a beat as I thought to myself, "Good, I have the place all to myself, just me and the Lord". I drove around to the back through a forest of beautiful tall trees. I love trees (you have to drive a very long way from Mesa Arizona, where I live now, to be in tall trees). I parked my van just as the ranger was making his rounds. He waved to me and off he went. Realizing he would probably not be back for a while, I bundled up my things and started walking towards the picnic table by the river.

I was going through some struggles with materialism. We lived in a very affluent area, and people based their self~esteem and identity on what car they drove, area and house they lived in and all sorts of other little trinkets, vacations and the like. I had eyed all of this in others, and I secretly desired more and more of this for myself.

I had been a Christian for about six years by then. I knew I was saved, I loved the Bible, church, and I definitely loved the Lord. But, I had one foot in the world and one foot in the Kingdom. He wanted me to move both of my feet over into the Kingdom of God.

I settled down on the bench seat at the picnic table, took out my Bible, turned to Ezekiel 16 and picked up where I had left off a few days prior. As I read, I came to verse 15. It walloped me hard as the Lord revealed to me His view of materialism. Wow! It says, "But, you trusted in your beauty and used your fame to become a prostitute." That was how He saw it. I tried exchanging the extremely harsh word prostitute, for worldly, because I figured I wasn't famous and I certainly never trusted in my beauty to get me anything. But the Lord still saw it differently. I was overwhelmed at my laczidazical attitude regarding something He wasn't taking lightly. The impact of this was rising in me, and my response was one I had never had with the Lord before.

I was brought to my knees right there beside the river. God's holiness just took my breath away. As the reverence and awe for the Lord soared, it reached to the point where I was face down on my stomach in the dirt. No other reaction would do. As I was humbled to the ground I could hear a sound that I hadn't taken notice of until that very moment. It was the sound of the mighty river at flood stage roaring in the background.

I was weeping and worshiping with all of my heart. I suddenly felt as though I had been extremely selfish in my relationship with God. At that very instant the Lord showed me that a relationship is two~sided.

So far my relationship with Him had been all about me. My salvation, my spiritual growth, my ministry, ME ME ME. WHAT ABOUT HIM! To love Him just because He is - His beautiful heart. When was I going to put my focus on Him? Just to love Him for Who He is!!

That day on my face trembling in the dirt with the water raging full force beside me I saw what it means to have a two~sided relationship.

He showed me that covenant is two~sided - a partnership.

That day in the park felt as if I had been re~reborn. I couldn't find words to describe what had happened. God would show me later in greater depth and detail His covenant, but at that moment I was just enthralled by Him. His love is wonderful, and His love for me astounds me more and more every day. Once I discovered this truth it changed my relationship with the Lord, I have this ache now for His presence — Him — for His heart. Not history, Bible wisdom, religion or church. All this is fine. But if this is all there is…

I have two questions for you to consider:

1. Are you a believer? - if not you are probably not having an awareness of a relationship with Him yet.
2. If you are a believer - is your relationship two-sided?

In other words, there are two ways to be lost.

1. You are not yet in a covenant relationship with Jesus.
2. You have lost your way; being concerned about Christian things but not completely alive with the joy of a true two-sided love.

It may take years to realize you are lost. Others may not see or notice that you are lost. You may even have the trappings of 'found-ness.'

1. You may be in church or church ministry.
2. You may be trying to follow all of the rules, but you are confused, soul weary, thirsty and tired, mimicking being alive but feeling dead inside.

The Lord wants you to have what's best. He wants you to have the fire of His presence filling you with passion and wonder and joy!!

After that day at the river, I began a 5-year adventure learning what my side of this two-sided relationship genuinely looks like. The Lord would have me discover what it means to worship Him. We will get back to this later in our study.

Fifth

Abraham was told he must 'keep' God's covenant - the action of his belief.

We notice this in Genesis 17:9:

"Then God said to Abraham, "As for you, you must keep my covenant, you and your descendants after you for the generations to come."

To seal the deal God told Abraham something extraordinarily unusual. Notice what it says in the next verse.

"...every male among you shall be circumcised. You are to undergo circumcision, and it will be the sign of the covenant between me and you."

What? At Abram's age, he must be circumcised. (Just in case you are not familiar with this term I encourage you to look it up in your dictionary.) A highly painful experience for any male baby but as an adult and before our modern technology, off the chart horrific. But, this was a crucial factor to God. Please place yourself right into this story. If Abraham had to be involved in this way, then you and I most certainly have our part as well.

With the cutting of circumcision, there is a scar that forms. The scar is the seal - the sign of the covenant. And every male in the household of every future generation of God's Hebrew people must be circumcised by the eighth day of their life.

What is the sign or seal of you being in covenant with God?

For the answer to this question read Ephesians 1:13-14:

_____

Now look at last week's lesson, step 6: How does circumcision fit as the scar?

_____

Look back at Genesis 17:13 & 14 and please fill in the blanks:

"My covenant _____ _____ _____ is to be an everlasting covenant."

What do you think this means?

_____

What happened if they did not obey?

_____

_____

Makes you think a bit doesn't it?

We conclude this week with this:

Please read Genesis 17:15 & 16:

Sarai received a new name too. What was hers? (notice the H) _____

Who would bear Abraham's covenant son? _____

They became the father and mother of many nations through their son Isaac -

In Genesis verses 20-22, what did God say would happen to Ishmael?

_____

_____

Challenge question - who are these people today? _____

(answer: the Arabs)

Fill in the blanks below from Genesis 17:21:

"But my covenant I will _____ with _____ , whom Sarah will bear to you by this time next year."

The promise revealed with a name and a date. What was the date?

_____

What were Abraham and Sarah told to name their son? _____

Before you conclude for this week, you may want to spend some time enjoying God's presence. There is absolutely nothing as beautiful as God's presence and glory! Has the Lord given you a more vivid and detailed view of Himself through a clearer lens? Celebrate and focus on what He has shown you this week. What appears as you process the picture?

Next week

We will pick up at Abraham's test with God. What was the test? Why was there a test? And did he pass the test?

Oh no, does this mean there is going to be a pop quiz for you?

Week 3

Pop Quiz

Last week

We studied the Abrahamic Covenant. Was your view of God brilliant as you hopefully gained a clearer more precise and vivid look straight into the heart of just how much God loves us? The fact that He would go to the trouble to create a covenant, let alone 'cut' covenant with us mere humans is incredible. But, remember the covenant was not actually 'cut' personally with Abram. God knew Abram would mess it up in some way, just as each one of us would have done in his shoes. God wisely cut the covenant with Himself. Now, think about it for a moment; does it surprise you at all that this huge essential detail is thought of by the Lord? More than that, God is holy, all powerful and glorious. He could only truly be in perfect covenant with Himself. That is what makes His total love for us even more inconceivable and marvelous!

This week

We are going to continue learning more about this particular covenant - the Abrahamic Covenant. Something very unusual had to happen in God's eyes for this to be complete. There is going to be a test. Don't fret the test is not for you, at least not at the moment. The test was for Abraham. But you may want to keep some notes because there may be a pop quiz at some point.

Getting Ready:

As you prepare for this week, please recall how you respond during tests. We keep this in the forefront of our mind while we dig deep into Abraham's pounding heart of emotion.

If you are part of a group study and therefore keeping up with your group but have not completed last week, you may want to work on that first. If you plunge into the middle of the story, you may not get as much out of it. However, I'm glad you are bringing this into your life in whatever way that looks and works for you. I'm excited for you as God reveals more of Himself to you. He is always good, and He loves us whether we study or not!!

Please write out our definition here. (You can look at the previous week if you can't remember.)

_____

_____

_____

First

Have you given any thought to the purpose of your life? To know what the reason is that you are here on the earth. Most people suppose it to be their life's career or maybe to fulfill a dream or calling. Some hope to find their perfect soul mate, get married, settle down and have children. Maybe for a few, it is to serve or help others by giving themselves to working for the homeless or prison ministry or going to a third world country to evangelize.

Many of us, including me, spend most of our lifetime agonizing over understanding this driving ambition. We could get through anything in life if we could just know what our purpose is. Right? It has taken me many years and gray hairs to come to realize that God is quite clear about our purpose. In fact, He put it in black and white in the Bible. For years I thought my purpose had to be some huge, profound, big eye-opener. In retrospect, God has been giving me the basic building block, and I have dismissed it as, 'not that profound'.

It has everything to do with the two-sided relationship we talked about last week. The key is intimacy with God or to put it another way, a relational encounter of walking with the Lord every step of our life and truthfully delving into our union of covenant with Him. Intimacy as a worshiper is the key has always been the key and is true life in the Lord. The 'big dream' that we keep trying to find is God Himself.

Paul, in the New Testament, describes it this way in the Amplified Bible, Philippians 3:10:

"My determined purpose is that I may know Him, that I may progressively become more deeply and intimately acquainted with Him, perceiving and recognizing and understanding the wonders of His Person."

Our purpose is made very clear in this passage, isn't it? The purpose of every believer, every single child of God, really every one of us is the same thing!! It is to know Christ Jesus.

So what does it mean to know someone? Please write down some of your thoughts below:

_____

_____

⇒ **To know means:** – to be cognizant of; to have a concept of in the mind through seeing, reading or hearing about.

For you to be certain of - to apprehend as true or factual - to be familiar with - to be sure about the identity of - to recognize (I know that voice) - to 'see God' - to have God reveal Himself to you.

There are some noteworthy words to take hold of in this Philippians 3:10 passage on the previous page.

1. This passage starts with what word? _____

Your decision and yours alone, and not even God will make this choice for you. There could be an empty feeling in your life at this moment if you have not made this choice.

God knows what your purpose is and if you determine to line up with that same purpose, you will, at the point of resolution, explode with true fulfillment!

2. That brings us to the next word in the verse, which is determined.

How would you describe this word: _____

_____

Do you have a dispute going on inside of yourself? Or are you determined? In life this can be towards anything; going on a diet, getting a job, working out, you name it. Unless we are determined, we will probably waste another year stuck on the same unfruitful path.

In this verse, we are referring to knowing the Lord. You see, God is determined that we know Him because this is His very best for us.

3. There is another definition for determination. You will love this...................covenant.

God is in determination/covenant with you. He is telling you He is determined to pursue you, and that He will never let up on that determination. He does not grow weary or tire of pursuing you. You are so significant and precious to Him.

He cut a blood covenant to show you His love for you!

4. Another word for determination is focus.

A focused life is one lived on purpose. Visualize a camel with those crazy blinders on either side of its eyes — it has to stay focused in one direction.

Focus   Focus   Focus

God is so worthy of all our focus and attention and adoration!

5. **Narrowing it down even further - focus relates to <u>worship</u>.**

Have you had times when your whole being was pinpointed right on God's indescribable Majesty? When was the last time that this happened? That is focus. You were swept up in worship.

Worship is worth-ship. (Tuck this away for later as we will get back to it in a future week.)

Review:

Determination = Covenant

Determination = Focus

Focus = Worship

The focus of our attention matters. What we pursue becomes the very center of our innermost core. Below is a short clipping of a section from our principal scripture passage for this study:

"...that you being rooted and established in love."

All of us have a vast root system in our thinking caused from our life situations, good or bad. God wants us to be rooted in His love (we are immediately rooted the minute we enter into covenant with God, but to know it or feel it is a process).

⇒ **Root means:** an underground portion from which anything derives origin. To give life or vigor - To take root, fix or implant - To be more firmly fixed or established.

(The opposite – the object loses its power when the root is gone)

I would like to share with you a snapshot of this process of forming the right root in my life:

When I was in the seventh grade, I tried out for cheerleader. I made the athletic portion but wasn't voted to the team through the popular vote. From that moment on I had a fixation on being popular. For some reason, this event was devastating and became a root that grew to entangle me.

God has His amazing way of working in our lives, and this is what He did:

A few years ago I went on a women's retreat to Williams Arizona at the Young Life camp. Lots of things were going on in my life at the time, and I was reluctant to go, but I was asked to put together a prayer walk. I struggled the entire weekend. It was perplexing to me as to why this was so excruciatingly difficult. This par-

ticular event was designed for women to bring their 'unchurched' friends, so the material was light, there was minimal corporate worship time, and there seemed to be an excessive amount of games. This type of situation has had a tendency to be a bit intimidating for me. I am a deep thinker, and I prefer to spend personal one on one time with people.

By the end of the weekend, I was a mess, fighting my flesh, grouchy and missing the riveting fellowship with the Lord and others I had gone there to enjoy. On the last day, I packed up my belongings and left the camp in my car. The other three women in my vehicle were yacking up a storm with each other, but I, on the other hand, pushed in a CD and spent the duration of the descent down the mountain singing, worshiping and communing with God. Eventually, the other women joined in with me. When we stopped for lunch one of them remarked, "We've got our Deb back."

The next morning I felt disappointed that there was no 'mountain top' experience. As I started my much needed time alone with the Lord, I was craving the Word, but it wasn't speaking to me. Exhausted and parched I felt defeated and upset. However, as I picked up my journal to start to write, I was taken aback by the overflow that followed….. volumes poured forth flooding onto the once empty pages. (I will spare you the lengthy version.)

I started out by writing, **"I am not the cheerleader type!"**

Funny!

I wrote…. "All these years since I didn't 'make' it as a cheerleader I have yearned for acceptance and desired to be included. The part of the weekend that was an enormous awakening was the moment I realized I am not dependent on fitting into this particular style of gathering. For me personally, it has an affinity to bring out emotions of feeling out of sorts, far away and distant from people."

"I was feeling left out and not included. I go to these strained and uncomfortable game settings and want to cower in the corner. It shrinks my spirit and makes my self~conscious neediness come out. I thought all these years I wanted to be a part of the leadership crowd all dressed in the 'outfit'. All this reminds me of the responses I had back in Jr. High."

<u>Not fitting in and not being popular!</u>

I saw how deep down this whole thing went……. The root was deep.

God showed me it is OK to be a serious, contemplative person and be free to be myself, who He made me to be and to rest in who I am in Him.

The astounding way God let me see this occurred on the Tuesday night before that women's retreat. Earlier in that day my daughter Andrea (12 at the time) came home off the school bus crying because her best friend Rafaela had joined the 'popular' girls and she felt excluded. Etched forever onto our family's heart is the name of the leader of the popular girls, **Morgan Klein**. Not because of her name but rather the symbolism that would unfold. As I consoled my daughter during that afternoon, she was still clearly upset, and as we grouped around the dinner table, she could not eat one bite of food. Her brother, Brian (18 at the time) in his 'infinite wisdom', told her, "You don't want to be a popular girl because they are stuck up." Then the pivotal moment happened as he exclaimed to her. "You don't want to be a **KLEINETTE**!" It took us a second but….We all finally got it and had to have a good laugh.

As I sat there engrossed in thought with the Lord that morning after the retreat, volumes of emotion were coming forth straight into that journal. Then suddenly. God conveyed to me, "You don't want to be a 'Kleinette' either! And for that matter a 'Morgan'." I began to see with new eyes how detrimental 'popular' had been in my life. I had yearned to be dressed up in the right outfit and to fit in when in reality I didn't even like any of that and never had.

I wrote. "I don't desire to be a cheerleader anymore! In fact, I see that I never did." Done deal! It seemed as though God had orchestrated that whole weekend just for me. I saw that the root of popular was enormous and intertwined with a lot of other lesser roots. I asked God to kill that strangling root – it was choking out any good roots He was trying to establish.

Then it came to me.

Rooted.

Wait a minute…

I've been intrinsically rooted in a need to be popular all the while God was wanting me to grasp Ephesians 3:17, that He had been growing another root, a bigger root.

THE ROOT OF HIS LOVE!

For many years the Lord has been growing a root of knowing who He is, in my covenant with Him. That root of understanding, along with an embedded knowing and feeling of His boundless love for me. is huge in me now! I have come to realize I am totally loved and I can rest in His love! And, I am in love – in love with the King!

(I want you to know that since this incident in my life the process is still ongoing. The Lord has taken me through a few more extremely painful trials and difficult tests that have wavered my trust at times - I believe this will be a continuing process for the duration of life here on earth)

This was the turning point.

The Lord brought to my heart one more imperative thought in all of this – God showed me, my place is not in seeking out the limelight to be popular, but instead, it is to be behind the scenes creating the mood and atmosphere for the King of Glory to be the most popular!!! **He is the popular one!**

I hope you can relate to my root of popular, I know we all struggle with wanting to be liked, otherwise referred to as people pleasing, co-dependency or however you want to phrase it.

What root or roots do you have and can identify in your own life?

_____

_____

As you keep learning and growing in your understanding of God's covenant of love, I hope you will see the exquisiteness of how the Lord works in your life to be rooted and established in love – Someone TOTALLY loves you!

Second

Last week, we left off with the promise of a son. 'This time next year' Sarah would give birth to a son, and Abraham and Sarah were to name him Isaac. I will give you a brief summary of some of the history that took place so you can be aware of the big event. In Chapter 21 of Genesis, the Lord was gracious to Sarah just as He had promised. **She became pregnant and gave birth to Isaac, Abraham's son.** When Isaac was eight days old, Abraham was obedient to the covenant, obeying God's command, circumcising him. Time went on, and Isaac grew to the age of an adolescent or young man.

Now we get to the big test. **Please read Genesis 22:1-5:**

Reread Genesis 22:1-2: If you will recall from last week Abraham slept through the covenant 'cutting'. His part, remember was to believe. To believe with his heart, down deep in his heart, in the part that only God can know. God wanted Abraham to know if his heart was indeed surrendered and given entirely to the Lord.

The test was to see if Abraham would be faithful to the covenant. Why do you think God required Abraham's part?

_____

It had to have seemed like a lifetime waiting for Isaac's birth and then after all those years; he was faced with the biggest trial of his life. Feelings had grown strong. Love had grown deep. His own flesh and blood, finally his promised son, the one he knew God had been speaking to him about all along. And now, God was asking him to make the sacrifice of the one thing that was the most valuable and beloved to him. How could Abraham do this?

Please read Genesis 22:2: Who did God ask Abraham to take? _____ _____

What was the name of his son? _____

How many sons does it say Abraham had? _____

Didn't Abraham also have Ishmael? Why do you think he was not included?

_____

What was it that God knew about Abraham's feelings? What three words did God use?

_____ _____ _____

You have just witnessed the very first time in all of Scripture that God used the word **love**. We do not see this keyword in print in the Bible until this precise moment. God chose to define Himself, with this word, right here, associating the word love to describe the intense feelings a father has for his son, especially his only son. God describes Himself this way in 1 John 4:8, **"God is love"**. I find this astounding!

In our human nature, we usually love someone because they are lovable; we live out of passion and emotion. The incredible truth is that God loves because love is who God is in His being. God's love has nothing to do with the object of His love – unlovable or loveable makes no difference. Love lies at the very core of God's nature. When that love touches you, there is nothing more powerful in all of the universe. He knows that when we intensely explore and come in contact with the depths of His love, we will never be the same. Nothing is stronger or more compelling than the Lord's love.

Where did God ask Abraham to take Isaac?

_____

How was he to know which mountain?

_____

Please look up 2 Chronicles 3:1: What place was this? What spot did God lead Abraham too?

_____ (also known as Mount Zion)

Go back again to Genesis 22:2: What did the Lord ask Abraham to do?

_____

Mount Moriah was where king Solomon, David's son, built the Temple. Amazing the coincidence? This was God's plan all along. Remember God told Abraham where to go. There would be a sacrifice on that mountain.

Abraham had only one son of the promise - he loved his son. Following through would demonstrate his genuine love for God. Wouldn't it?

Please read Genesis 22:3: What is the first word of **verse 3**? _____

What does this word indicate about Abraham's willingness?

_____

Whom and what did he take for the journey?

1. _____

2. _____

3. _____

4. _____

Do you see that Abraham followed God's instructions, not his emotions? _____

Please read Genesis 22:4-5: How did Abraham discover the place he was to go to?

_____

He looked up! Eyes to heaven! Ready to hear from God!

What did he tell the servants?

_____

_____

From the words of Abraham in **verse 5**, what is the most interesting fact that he stated? Such faith!

_____

He included Isaac on the return back down from the mountain. And to Abraham, it was all about worship…

Third

We continue to discover what happened to Isaac. **Please read Genesis 22:6-14:**

Please reread verses 6 and 7:

The wood for the burnt offering was placed on whom? _____

Who carried the fire and the knife? _____

Isaac speaks up here what did he say?

_____

Please read verse 8:

While we unravel what Abraham said it is crucial to think on and remember this statement as we dig deeper into the New Covenant. Abraham was confident when he said that, "God Himself will provide the lamb for the burnt offering, my son." I discovered that in another Bible translation it says, "God will provide Himself for the burnt offering." Do you see the magnitude of these words?

"Behold the Lamb of God, which takes away the sin of the world." John 1:29

Below write out John 3:16:

_____

_____

Abraham believed in God and His promises. He was convinced that the Lord would come through on his behalf. He trusted! Abraham moved forward, one step at a time. He followed the instructions not his emotions. Sometimes our greatest expressions of love are through our actions, not our emotional responses. He kept his focus on the most important One. He built an altar, arranged the wood, and bound his son, who somehow went along with this willingly. Can you imagine? What incredible love is revealed and shown in Isaac as well and what undeniable trust.

Abraham placed his only beloved son on top of the wood.

Please read verse 10:

Abraham obediently reached for the knife to slay his son. Think about this. Really think about it. Could you do this? I didn't think so. Why in the world does it seem as though Abraham had so much more faith, courage, love and definitely more belief in God, than either of us do? Does it seem that way to you? It does to me. It had to be God's grace! God's grace was sufficient for this requirement. What I realized is that God's grace is sufficient for each of us uniquely as we venture through our own personal trials (thankfully we don't have to go through Abraham's unique situation — just our own).

Now we come to **verse 11.** Who called out to Abraham from heaven?

_____

What was said in **verse 12**?

_____

_____

God steps in. Right at Abraham's darkest moment, God steps in.

What did the Lord know about Abraham's heart? How?

_____

_____

He was true to the covenant. He was determined. Remember that all of this was for one purpose, to test Abraham to see if he would be faithful to the covenant he slept through. Remember this is a two-sided relationship. Abraham needed someone to stand in for him (Jesus was his substitute). Even though he definitely had his personal involvement.

We can see that he was indeed faithful in keeping his 'side' of the covenant. He passed the test!!!

Come with me and see how perfectly God provided as He stepped in:

Please read verse 13:

What was in the thicket? _____   _____

What did it just so happen to be caught by? _____   _____

This is a foreshadowing of Jesus' history changing event. A thicket is a thorn-bush. Jesus was the ram or Lamb whose holy head was crowned with a wreath of thorns. And Jesus is the horn of our salvation. God did provide Himself!!!

And, Abraham's necessary sacrifice did take place. As he was climbing the mountain on one side, God had His provision climbing the mountain on the other side. Eventually, when the timing was right, God revealed what was demanded. The required ram was provided for Abraham.

The ultimate fulfillment of the New Covenant was provided, at just the right time too. Jesus the Lamb of God! God, as Jesus, provided Himself as the Lamb for the burnt offering. At this same location on Mount Moriah. Maybe even the exact same spot! High up on the mountain in Jerusalem!

What did Abraham name this place in **verse 14**?_____

Fourth

Let's look at some aspects of what Abraham went through, what he believed and also what we believe, in our covenant relationship.

We look at what Abraham believed:

1. First, he believed in a supernatural birth. The son in his old age after there seemed to be no hope. Isaac was his miracle.
2. He obeyed the covenant and had his son circumcised on the eighth day.
3. Abraham believed that through his seed all the nations of the world would be blessed.
4. Somehow he had enough faith in God to offer his only son as a sacrifice, whatever the outcome.
5. He was also certain that God would provide a substitute sacrifice, either that or raise his son from the dead because he stated that they would both be coming back down the mountain together – alive.

What are we asked to believe:

1. First, we are asked to believe in a supernatural birth. The virgin birth of Jesus through the Holy Spirit.
2. We are to believe in the Jewish sign of covenant in that Mary and Joseph had Jesus circumcised on the eighth day. The Bible confirms this.
3. The Bible says that Jesus is the Seed from Abraham's genealogy.
4. We know through Scripture that Jesus, in joy, ascended the mountain knowing the fate that would be His destiny. This is the very same mountain - showing God kept His promise.
5. The one thing, our belief, is what brings us into covenant with God—that God Himself (in Jesus) laid Himself on the altar (the cross).
6. Jesus was raised to life.

Consider this thought –

What kind of Father could satisfy the need for justice with the death of His own Son? Wasn't there another way? Couldn't He forgive but not have to carry it out in exactly this uniquely unusual way? We don't want to miss the purpose of the cross. It was not some need to be satisfied at God's Son's expense. Instead, it was a need that we each have, our sin nature, that must be forgiven. This was done at God's own expense because of His unfailing love. At the cross, He provided the undeniable proof of just how much He loves us.

It is interesting that this is actually a trust issue. **Do we truly believe that God's love is the love of a Father?**

Fifth

Here is the place for **YOUR POP QUIZ**!

Like Abraham, are we faithful to the covenant? Determined?

Your part, remember, is to believe. To believe with your heart, down deep in your heart, in the part that only God can know. God wants you to know if your heart is indeed surrendered, given completely to Him. So it's fascinating if you think about it... does it seem as though God tests you. (Have you ever needed to know the answers to the quiz and to see personally for yourself that you passed. Why take the quiz yet never find out?)

Abraham obeyed God even though he was finally a father and this was his precious son. But it was more than that; he trusted God too. We can obey God yet not trust Him and miss out on the two-sided relationship with Him.

God undoubtedly wants us to relate to Him in love rather than obey Him from fear. God knows that love can flourish only where there is real trust.

Abraham called that place 'God will provide'.

Do you trust God that He has already provided, the perfect needed sacrifice - His One and Only Son, Jesus Christ! When you said yes to Jesus, you entered into covenant with Him. Remember it's a two-sided relationship. Just as God has His part, so do you, to do the mighty work of believing – you are a 'believer'. If you think this is simple, I wonder whether you are seeing that there have been some pop quizzes and probably also some emotionally draining tests!

Let's look at our hearts –

The love between God and Abraham and Abraham and God was covenant love. This is the most sacred, special, enduring, binding, and close bond between two people. As a child of God, you are also in this **LOVE**.

There is a question that seems to elude many wonderful people of faith. That question is- Do 'you' personally **FEEL THIS LOVE**? It is one thing to intellectualize, this love. However, encountering love is when it sinks from your head to your heart, and you truly **FEEL LOVED**. Then your life changes.

You can say – "I know I am loved by the King!"

But there still remains one more question in this love.

In the Gospel of John, John 21:15-19, Jesus asks Peter a question that I think is extremely compelling. Jesus asks Peter, **"Do you love Me?"** Interesting that He would even ask that question at all.

Think about this question. God cares about being loved!!

"Do you love Me?"

I was a homemaker for 22 years and loved it. I love to decorate and do interior design. I have always taken great pride in my house being a home, clean and beautiful, fun and full of love.

We purchased a home in Arizona at the peak of the market. After living in it for a little over a year, we realized we were in over our head. We decided to put our house on the market. It was on the golf course with a gorgeous view of Red Mountain so we figured it would sell quickly. All of our other houses in California had sold in one week or less. I had no idea what we were going to go through. Months and months and months went by. Model home perfect gets old really quick. That was a time that left me feeling vulnerable and afraid. Every night I went to bed it was one less day of money we had left in our bank account to sustain the continuous out-going flow of cash (did I mention my husband was without a job?).

An increase in panic led to feelings of dejection, "God will You come through for me?"

One morning the Lord set Mark 4:35-41 before me. A familiar passage to me but as I read it in that intense moment, I could feel myself relating and seeing God in it. A big storm and Jesus was sleeping in the back of the boat. The disciples woke Him and asked the question, ***"Teacher don't you care if we drown?"***

I felt it.

I felt the persistent gnawing of this in me.

From my journal:

"I'm drowning in over my head, sinking, gasping for breath, help, help, help me. Jesus, our family will sink soon. We can't rescue ourselves. Throw us a life raft or come to us Yourself. Nothing in life matters with all this stress."

I felt like I was losing my mind and all the while I felt God asking me this one question over and over....

"Do you love Me?"

For almost a year He asked me this question. In the midst of all this on-going panic in my heart.

"Do you love Me?"

"I can say I love you Lord, but way down deep when I have no inkling of feeling blessed and I wonder if You 'care if we drown', Lord, do I love you in THIS? Regardless of anything else. This is truly the question. I hesitate to answer it tritely because, Lord, I know you know my thoughts and my motives because You know me. Truthfully I am not sure of Your total love for me, where do I fit in with You? This is making it hard to be sure. I have always thought I loved You so much Lord that no matter what I would go through it would never affect that love – I could do anything for You. But now, do I believe what I think I know of You? Is it thoroughly embedded and rooted down in me, down deep?"

I knew faith had something to do with it – faith proved genuine.

"Do you love Me?"

A crisis of faith! I sensed that this would radically change me. Fully persuaded of His love. This is a level of faith and love I don't yet know.

"Put your house on the altar – Lay it down."

Months more.....

In the middle of the night, I came to the end of myself and the end of my rope in regards to the house and the end of doubting God on HOW He would provide.

I finally trusted His will, over mine.

One after the other the Lord has asked me to lay **this** and **that Isaac** on the altar.

How about you? What Isaacs have you had to lay on the altar?

_____

What are you going through right now? What crisis of faith?

_____

_____

God did show up for Abraham and me, as the rescuer and Savior and as the 'one who cares if we drown'. Through this, I learned He knows what is **BEST** for me.

He is asking us, **"Do you love Me?"**, not because He doesn't know the answer, but He is asking, so **we** will know the answer. The answer comes in direct correlation to being rooted and established in **love**. Do we know how wide and long and high and deep is the love of God? If we want to have a love for Jesus, we must study hard Jesus' love for us.

Being "Fully Persuaded" would become a journey for me.......

> **"Yet I am not ashamed, because I know whom I have believed, and am convinced that he is able to guard what I have entrusted to him for that day." 2 Timothy 1: 12**

I love You, Lord!

You are beautiful! I sing praises to Your Name! You are glorious!

Feel free to **journal** any thoughts or emotions you have toward the Lord and Savior, your Covenant Partner.

Next week

Excitement is building, and I assure you that what you learn is going to change your perspective on life. We pick up with Moses. You will see God's faithfulness to His people as He guided them on their journey. Your soul will be simply riveted to the grand details of God's plan.

Week 4
Simply Riveted

Last week

We journeyed to the center of the covenant, the test. To God, this may have been the most important part. He asks the question, **"Do you love Me?"**, Not because He is in 'need' of our love, but it is because He sincerely desires to be loved. Would Abraham's heart be completely given to Him? Would he do absolutely anything for his Covenant Partner? We saw that Abraham did, in fact, pass the test. He willingly took one step at a time to offer his beloved only son, Isaac, as a sacrifice. He obediently followed through with the act of 'cutting' covenant right up to the second when God intervened at just the right moment with a substitute sacrifice. Abraham had incredible faith! And what incredible love he demonstrated!

You were confronted with a pop quiz, but only on paper, certainly nothing quite as real as Abraham. But to the Lord, it is just as real. Where is your heart? God stepped in at just the right moment with the perfect, spotless substitute sacrifice for you as well.

This week

Excitement is building, and I assure you that what you learn is going to change your perspective on life. And you will come to understand even more astounding details of God's wonder. We will briefly summarize the events that took place between the time of Abraham and Moses. You'll be a witness to the love that God had, and has for His people, as He guided, watched over and kept all of His promises. The Lord not only makes promises, but He alone has the power to keep and perform them 100% of the time. He is always consistent and faithful.

You will be drawn into the adventurous life of Moses. We sometimes hear about his extraordinary life in fragmented pieces that over many years are glued together in one sermon or another. This week you will be riveted and moved as you come right along side of Moses and experience his adventure through the response and sentiment of your own heart. Once you see the significance of the plagues, especially the 10th one, there will be a permanent connection in your soul as to why the 10 plagues shook not only the nation of

Israel, but also the whole Egyptian territory. This, in turn, will help you grasp what Passover is and why it is pivotal in every one of our lives, whether we are aware of it or not?

Getting Ready:

As you open God's holy Word, you may want to stop and take a moment to tell your Lord and King something wonderful you know to be true of Him. Thank Him for His Word, ask the Holy Spirit to teach you and counsel you in the inner sanctuary of your soul. Rest in God - rest in His glorious presence!

The last two days of this week are the most poignant, so if you are running short on time, you may want to invest more effort in the later half. But I assure you that it will be a blessing, and it will make more sense to you if you do it in its entirety.

Let's define covenant:

This time write out in **YOUR OWN WORDS** what covenant means and what it means to you personally.

_____

_____

_____

First

I have put together a short summary loaded with specific abbreviated chronological events and family history that will help you organize and categorize things in your mind.

Please read this slowly and thoughtfully:

We know Abraham had Isaac...

... And Isaac had Jacob — whom God renamed Israel. (God continued the covenant reminder with a name change (Gen 35:10)). Jacob/Israel had 12 sons (the 12 tribes of Israel) (Gen 35:23-36). All of the Hebrew people descended from one of these 12 tribes. One of Jacob's sons was Joseph, whom he favored. His other sons were jealous of Joseph, so they sold him into slavery and then lied to their father explaining that he had been killed by an animal (Gen 37:12-36).

Joseph ended up in Egypt in Potiphar's household. He went to prison because he refused to sleep with Potiphar's wife, who tried to seduce him and then accused him of rape (Gen 39:6-20). In prison, he was recognized and favored as he was called upon to interpret dreams for Pharaoh (Gen 41:25-40). Pharaoh eventually placed Joseph in charge over the land of Egypt (Gen 41:41).

A severe famine came upon the land, and Jacob's (Israel's) sons unexpectedly discovered that the brother they had sold many years before, was now second in command over Egypt. Even though Joseph experienced many painful, challenging and grave problems he was an overcomer and grew to be a mighty man of

God. A caring, merciful man who did not allow bitterness or resentment to control his opinion or demeanor toward his brothers. And because of this, the entire nation of Israel moved to Egypt where they were favored and blessed because of Joseph's relationship with Pharaoh.

We have summed up the end of the book of Genesis, and we pick up at the beginning of Exodus. Time has passed, and Joseph has died, so have all of his brothers, and the Pharaoh too. A new Pharaoh, who did not know Joseph came into power in Egypt. He became nervous that the Israelites were becoming too numerous and feared a rise in their influence, he put slave masters over them to oppress them. He used forced labor (brick and mortar laying) to undermine their strength.

We will stop here and look up Exodus 1:22. Write out what it says below:

_____

_____

_____

There was a boy named Moses who was born during the time of this order. His mother hid him for 3 months. And an unusual sequence of unique circumstances led to Moses' divine protection. His mother sent him out into the Nile River in a basket with her own daughter, Moses' sister, watching over him. Concurrently Pharaoh's daughter went down to the river to bathe. She discovered Moses crying among the reeds and felt sorry for him even though she knew he was one of the Hebrew babies. Going against her father's edict, she carried out her notion of holding onto him for herself. So Moses was allowed to live when he should have been killed.

Moses was raised in the royal household of Pharaoh. Throughout his youth, he was privy to his true lineage and heritage. But later in is young adult life he overheard 2 Egyptian men maligning the Israelites and in his anger, he killed one of them. It turned out that this act was observed by a witness who threatened to reveal his secret. So in a state of panic Moses fled to Midian where he lived for 40 years. In this new territory, he eventually married Zipporah a Midianite, and she gave birth to their first son.

The Burning Bush:

We are now at the inception of Moses' journey with God. At this point in our study, I would like for you to allow yourself to become engaged with the real life drama. We go to many movies that seem to have a strange way and the intention of bringing our emotions to a peak. As we are championing for our favorite lead character, we often find ourselves rooting for them by the conclusion of the film. I would like you to let yourself get engrossed into Moses' position and role in a similar way.

Please read Exodus 3:1-10:

In the ordinary mundane tasks of the day Moses had his first encounter with God. The Lord made His initial appearance to Moses in flames of fire within a bush, and somehow the bush was not consumed. Sensational!

Moses had heart-pounding fear. Can you imagine this occurring in your own life — maybe as you are walking your dog at the park?

God reconfirmed His covenant as we note in verse 6. God was concerned about the misery and suffering of His people because of their slave/task masters. He said He had come down to rescue them and give them the land He had promised to Abraham.

What was the description of this land in verse 8?

_____

Remember God promised them Canaan, but not until after they would be enslaved for 400 years (if you recall this was foretold while Abram was in that deep sleep). This hill country of Canaan was described as a good and spacious land, a land flowing with milk and honey. The Promised Land!

After 400 years, it is finally time!

Verse 10 says, **"So now, go. I am sending you to Pharaoh to bring my people the Israelites out of Egypt."**

Who was God referring to with the word 'you'? _____

What if this were you?

Moses couldn't see himself in this role either...

Moses protested 5 different times to God:

- **The first time** - was in **Exodus 3:11**. Moses asked God, "Who am I? ...", and God answered him with "I will be with you."

- **The second time** - was in **verses 3:13-14**. Moses wanted to know what to answer the Israelites when they asked, "What is His name? Then what shall I tell them?" God answered him with, "I AM WHO I AM... I AM has sent me (Moses) to you."

- **The third time** - was in **Exodus 4:1-9**. Moses questioned God with, "What if they do not believe me...?" God answered him in advance telling him what miraculous signs he would perform (staff into a snake, hand with leprosy, and water from the Nile to turn into blood).

- **The fourth time** - was in **verse 4:10**. Moses told God, "O Lord, I have never been eloquent ... I am slow of speech and tongue." God answered him with, "Who gave man his mouth?"

- **The fifth time** - was in **Exodus 4:13**.

What did Moses say in complete reluctance?_____

What was the Lord's answer to him? (Exodus 4:14-16)

_____

_____

Most of us do not think we are eloquent.

Have you ever protested about speaking on God's behalf? What was His answer to you?

_____

_____

The idea of getting up in front of people and having to articulate competently, be poised, and have something of value to share, has scared the living daylights out of me. My two greatest fears are - having a loved one die and public speaking.

I remember the thought of opening up and sharing with other women in a small Bible study, oh how this terrified me. Then one day the Lord appointed me to lead one of those small groups. As I got up the nerve, the day came when I was asked to emcee a mother-daughter tea. I had to ad-lib and be spontaneous with little girls who were fidgety. I survived mainly because I had great support from a few loving women who conscientiously bolstered and propped me up. However, I honestly think they were thankful it wasn't them.

My next big adventure the following year was to be the evening speaker at a women's ministry dinner. My topic was 'Friendship'. Now looking back, I think this was a bit ironic since I hadn't learned anything about covenant yet. I just expounded on – 'If you want to have friends you have to be a good friend.'

God promoted me (not sure it was an upgrade) to weekend workshop speaker, then to a keynote weekend speaker. All of this was in the progression of His grace. My most exhilarating moment would have to be my first co-ed venture. I remember telling the large group, of predominantly men, that I was visualizing them in wigs and lipstick. Public speaking hasn't reached the easy stage for me yet, my nerves still feel frayed, and I am often edgy until I stand up on the 'platform' and begin. I have to say I have at least addressed my fear, and it doesn't seem to be as right in my face scary now.

Like Moses, I had to learn to let the Lord do the talking through me.

The one aspect of speaking that has never rattled me is that of praying in front of people, even large crowds. Because in prayer I am really only talking to an audience of One.

Moses did obey God! It took him awhile, though. (Doesn't this make you feel better that even Moses had trouble with his faith and obedience?) Just as with Moses, God keeps giving us new opportunities, and He keeps giving us His answer.

Moses headed back to Egypt taking the staff of God with him **(Exodus 4:17)**.

"...take this staff in your hand so you can perform miraculous signs with it."

Miraculous signs, what??

Please read Exodus 4:21 and answer the next two questions:

What was Moses's first assignment when he arrived in Egypt?

_____
_____

What was the startling thing that God did to Pharaoh?

_____

God is completely sovereign!!! Does He control even the heart. What are your thoughts on this?

_____

Second

I want to backtrack for just a couple of verses so we can benefit from detecting what God said to Israel **before** anything would ever transpire.

Please read Exodus 3:18-21:

I love how God works and how He shows us His work. He told Moses exactly what 'would' happen. In other words He gave prior prophecy and evidence of the coming plagues. The Lord told Moses and the elders of Israel to go to Pharaoh and tell him what in **verse 18**?

_____
_____

Notice it says they were to journey into the desert. What does **verse 19** foretell?

_____

Describe **verse 20**?

_____

God told them exactly what was going to take place. God is omniscient. He knows all. In verse 21 God also said that when they were released into the desert they would not go empty-handed. Keep this in your mind not only for these Israelites but also for yourself as well. God will provide!

The tension is mounting as we begin to see the reason for the plagues:

Go forward to where we left off in Exodus 4:22-23 and write out these two verses below:

_____

_____

You may have heard about this verse before, "Let my people go!!"

My daughter's sixth-grade class did a skit on stage 'performing' this song.

Have you ever heard it?

CHORUS: Pharaoh, Pharaoh
Oh, baby, let my people go.
OOH, AAH, Yeah, Yeah, Yeah, Yeah (REPEAT)

It was based on the song 'Louie Louie' and written by Richard Berry in 1955. It was recorded in 1963 and became popular in the 1980's. It even has specific hand motions and various grunts. (It's worth watching on YouTube — find one with the hand motions it will make you laugh!)

I noticed that there is more to this than just being let go out of Egypt. Do you see it? What does the rest of **verse 23** say — what were they to do?

_____

Did you ever notice that until now?

They were to sacrifice; they were to exalt the Lord; they were to **worship**!!

The verses state that Israel was God's firstborn son, representing collectively all of the Israelites — their special covenant relationship with God. It is shocking to see in **verse 23** that God told them what would happen to Pharaoh's firstborn son. What was going to happen to him?

_____

Please read these puzzling verses in Exodus 4:24-26:

In these verses there is a very critical point that is made about Moses' disobedience to the covenant. Right here right now at this pivotal moment the Lord was about to kill Moses (without warning?). Why do you think God would do this to His beloved child?

_____

This was part of the covenant. Moses was in breach of his part. God took this seriously. Part of the deep love of the Lord is to help keep Moses' mistake from causing him harm.

The blood covenant was sacred and binding. We see that Moses' wife Zipporah quickly performs a circumcision on their son and Moses' life was spared.

Moses and Aaron finally proceed to go before Pharaoh.

Read Exodus 5:1-7. In verse 1 what did they go and tell Pharaoh God said?

_____

Notice the mention again of going out into the desert to worship. Your translation may say to hold a festival. Festivals or Feasts were times of sacrifice, fasting and celebrating God. What did Pharaoh say about the Lord in **verse 2**?

_____

Was Pharaoh willing to comply? _____

Do you think this made a difference in God's plan? _____

The Lord will have the final word showing Pharaoh exactly who He is and just how powerful.

In Exodus 5:6-7 Pharaoh's strong will and hard heart caused him to increase the Israelites labor burden by requiring them to make the same number of bricks, but now they would have to supply their own straw.

Bewildered, Moses returned to the Lord (in Exodus 5:23) wondering why God had not rescued them from all their torment. Would God be faithful to His covenant people?

In Exodus 6:6 it says, **"Therefore, say to the Israelites: 'I am the Lord, and I will bring you out from under the yoke of the Egyptians. I will free you from being slaves to them, and I will redeem you with an outstretched arm and with mighty acts of judgment."**

God promised to:

1. Bring them out from under the yoke of the Egyptians.
2. Free them from being slaves under their oppression.
3. **Redeem** them with an outstretched arm and with mighty acts of judgment.

It is interesting that this is the first time in the Bible for the word **redeem**.

⇒ **Redeem means:** to regain possession of by paying a price, to receive back, to set free, rescue, or ransom. To rescue from sin and its penalties.

God would fulfill His oath and promise.

Third

Moses and Aaron trusted God and did entirely and precisely what He commanded them to do.

Moses took up the staff:

The battle has begun (spoiler alert - we already know who won). God was releasing His people from their seemingly endless captivity. There would be a price to get set free as all of the ten plagues were horrendous calamities, and they increased in their intensity. Notice below that some plagues impacted everyone and everything around them while other plagues differentiated between certain people or animals or places. (In bold below.)

Plague 1   Plague of blood - Nile River turned to blood. Every stream, pond, and bucket of water. The fish died which left a great stench.

Plague 2   Plague of Frogs - Aaron stretched out his hand over the waters, frogs came and covered the land. Frogs everywhere even in beds.

Plague 3   Plague of Gnats - As the rod struck the dust the dust became gnats or insects like lice.

Plague 4   Plague of Flies - Dense swarms of flies poured out **only** on Pharaoh's palace and all of the Egyptians houses but **not** on the Israelites' homes.

Plague 5   Plague on Livestock - All the animals owned by the Egyptians died **but not** the livestock belonging to the Israelites.

Plague 6   Plague of Boils - Soot from a furnace was tossed into the air, and festering boils broke out on the Egyptian men and animals.

Plague 7   Plague of Hail - Moses stretched out his hand toward the sky and hail fell all over Egypt, the worst storm on the nation of Egypt. It **did not** hail on Goshen where the Israelites were.

Plague 8   Plague of Locusts - Wind brought locusts in huge numbers covering the ground until it was black. They devoured all the vegetation, nothing green remained.

Plague 9   Plague of Darkness - Total darkness covered all of Egypt for three days, a darkness that could be **felt**. Yet, all the Israelites had light in the places where they lived.

Pharaoh was outraged! Moses was exiled from Pharaoh's sight never to appear before him again!

What's next? How did this help the Israelites get out of Egypt?

Fourth

I want to commend you for an accomplished job working through all of this history! Wasn't it outstanding to see God's faithfulness and His incredible power and authority? Emerging from these plagues rises up the unfolding, and unpacking of very specific symbolism foreshadowing the cross and how we are **redeemed**. It was the precursor to seeing the full redemption brought about through our Lord Jesus Christ. God redeemed the Israelites from their bondage in Egypt through the 10th Plague.

> **Plague 10**   Plague of the Firstborn

This reading in Exodus 11:1-7 is important. What was it that the Lord told Moses in verses 4 & 5? Please write it out below in your own words:

_____
_____
_____

Sounds a little like what we observed Pharaoh give as orders back in Exodus 1:22:

"Then Pharaoh gave this order to all his people:
'Every boy that is born you must throw into the Nile, but let every girl live.'"

According to **Exodus 11:7** would any harm come to the Israelites? _____

Who would go throughout Egypt to kill the firstborn sons, look back at **verse 4**?_____

Did you see that? In what ever way you want to perceive this, God had a plan to protect them. His love always prevails and protects. His plan had more to it, though. Far reaching glory!!

Throughout the remainder of the years of history, all the way up to the death of Jesus, the Jewish people were to observe this festival each and every year. We find out what God's protection **required** of the Israelites (remember their side of the two-sided covenant). Each year they were to observe this as a festival or feast to remind them of God's redemption. They had to follow vital and life-saving requirements described in detail giving very specific instructions down to the day and time.

Although this may come across to you as a bit ritualistic or even legalistic, I would ask you instead to...

Visualize yourself as one of the members of this community. We have traditions that we pass down from one generation to the next, but often we have no idea how or why they even got started in the first place. But the Hebrew people had a very definite purpose and intention for why they would keep this tradition.

I want to remind you that God's protection was for the **whole community** of Israel. That **each man**, as in everyone, with no one exempt, were to partake in God's provision. If they did not participate, they were left out from under God's protective umbrella. You may have thought this was just for the Israelites. However...

As it is written: "**There is no one righteous, not even one; ...**" Romans 3:10

Read Exodus 12:1-7:

The calendar of events is critical. The exact times at the exact dates must be completely obeyed and observed.

What was the month? _____

What was the day? _____

The first month of the Jewish calendar, the month of Nisan.

What was each head of the household to do on that day? What if your family was too small for a whole lamb?

_____

_____

Notice again that **each** member of the family was to eat the lamb.

Describe the animal below.

_____

_____

In **verse 6** what was to happen to the animal and for how many days?

_____

They were to observe it, to make sure that there was no spot or blemish, to 'find no fault' with the lamb.

What were they to do with the blood in **verse 7**?

_____

Blood was the sign - the way out from under the plague or the curse. The blood. Only if you had the blood. We've toned down this teaching (so here I am to preach it to you).

There are only two kinds of people:

Those who **HAVE THE BLOOD** and those who **DON'T HAVE THE BLOOD**. The blood of the lamb in this Exodus passage was a sign or shadow type of Jesus Christ the Lamb. Jesus' death completed and fulfilled our blood requirement and our rescue forever.

Blood is life. An example in the case of our bodies is that our blood delivers oxygen and nutrition to our cells. Without it, our limbs and organs die. We all need the life-giving power of our blood. In the absence of this blood, we have no life.

The blood was the only protection:

It was the mercy – literally the mercy from death. The blood is still the only protection for the forgiveness of sins and the mercy from death. We've learned many things in our churches but sometimes fail to learn about the blood, therefore, we have people who do not feel they are forgiven.

Do you have the blood?

Without it, you have no proof of your son-ship/covenant. Through it, you have complete access to your spiritual inheritance. (If you are in covenant, you have the blood.) Strength and vitality, plus all the promises and blessings of God flow to you through the blood of Jesus the Lamb. Precious Jesus!!

Way back when I was a very impressionable young Christian, and a mom with young children, I was at a retreat in the redwoods at Mt. Hermon Conference Center in California. I don't remember the speaker or the topic. but I will never forget how Communion that last day impacted and altered my soul forever. Gut wrenching emotion. a lump in my throat and tears streaming down my cheeks. I took Communion for the first time riveted in a new awareness of the Lord's sacrifice. His love overwhelmed me. This experience began as one of the women at the retreat got up and read a story about a mother and young daughter who were trapped for days in the rubble after an earthquake shook their city. I was engulfed with the following...

(by Max Lucado, Chapter 2 of <u>When God Came Near</u>)

"Mommy, I'm so thirsty. I want a drink."

It was then I remembered I had my own blood."

Her groping finger, numb from the cold, found a piece of shattered glass. She sliced open her left index finger and gave it to her daughter to suck. The drops of blood weren't enough. "Please, Mommy, some more. Cut another finger." Susanna has no idea how many times she cut herself. She only knows that if she hadn't, Gayaney would have died. Her blood was her daughter's only hope.

Engulfed in the thought and the feelings of that kind of intense human love and realizing the magnitude of the loving sacrifice of Jesus, I was caught up in the thought, Jesus' blood is life!

Fifth

Why is all of this vivid description so vital for you to be able to see the total plan of God's incredible covenant? There are no coincidences with God. Every detail is absolutely necessary.

Please reread Exodus 12:6-7:

They had to kill the lambs at what hour in order to have all the preparations done on time?

Twilight, between sunset and nightfall. They had to eat the lamb by 6 o'clock in the evening.

Are you putting yourself into this explicit drama? You are there at that moment grabbing a branch of hyssop to apply the blood to the doorframes of your 'house' in unison with each Israelite family. Hyssop is a plant or reed that is full of water. It has a hairy surface that is good to hold liquids. When this plant was dipped into the blood, both water and blood were being applied to the doorframes.

"Cleanse me with hyssop, and I will be clean wash me, and I will be whiter than snow." Psalm 51:7

They had applied the blood to the doorframes with the hyssop. Now, please draw your attention to the fact that **each** member of the family had to enter their house through the blood-stained door. They walked through the door. They entered **in** to be spared, the door to safety!

"Jesus said again, "I tell you the truth, I am the gate (door) for the sheep." John 10:7

"I am the gate (door); whoever enters through me will be saved." John 10:9

Please read the above scriptures again. Do you see it? Jesus declared Himself the door.

Jesus is the door of safety. He is making the offer to everyone to enter in and be spared. Jesus is the only doorway to eternal life. There is only one way into the Kingdom of heaven. It is not through your church membership nor is it your genealogy. Religion is not the door. Baptism is not the door nor are your good deeds. In fact, it is easy to go through a door, but a door is only helpful if it is sourced correctly. Jesus is our Source of life. Glorious, marvelous Jesus!

Once inside their houses, they prepared the lamb and ate it. What are God's specifications for preparing the meal?

Answer the following questions after you read Exodus 12:8-11:

How was the meat prepared? **Circle the correct answer.** Was it?

Raw   Cooked in water   Roasted over fire

Were they allowed to have leftovers? And what were they to do with them?

_____

Describe what they were to wear and how they were to eat? Were they to dine by candlelight or like our 'fast food'?

_____

Why do you think the Lord had them eat it this way?

_____

How many of the animal's bones could be broken? (the answer is in **Exodus 12:46**) _____

Have you ever wondered why these particular steps and traditions are known as Passover?

It appears obvious but…Passover got its name because death would literally **pass over** those specific houses that had the blood. So this day was called Passover.

This will be the sign:

Please read Exodus12:12-13:

What did God tell Moses and Aaron that He would do in **verse 12**?

_____

Who did God say He would bring judgment upon?

_____

Again what would be the sign in **verse 13**?

_____

What would God do when He saw this sign?

_____

What was God's promise in **verse 13**?

_____

OK, we have that straight, and the facts are clear. But are they?

1) Please note that in this last verse it **DOES NOT SAY** that 'No destructive plague will touch you when I strike the Egyptians'. What does it say?

_____

2) Many who are familiar with this story assume that the blood on the doors was a sign for the Angel of Death. But notice the curious detail in this scripture.

The Lord said to Moses, **"... I am the Lord. The blood (of the Passover lamb) will be a sign for you on the houses where you are; and when I see the blood, I will pass over you." (Exodus 12:13)**

Although the Lord was looking for the blood on the door, and when He saw it He would pass over each house, the blood was **NOT** a sign for Him.

It says quite clearly that the blood was a 'sign for you' – the people. (And by extension, it is a sign for all of us who read this.) What is a sign?

Signs are pointers. They are not there to direct us to the sign itself but something else. The sign was established *by* God – He's the author of it. So just as with any other sign, what did He want to show us?

It is remarkable that the **timing** of the sacrifice of the lambs on Passover was the exact same day of the year and the exact same time of day, but, many years later in which Jesus went to the cross. This sign was mainly there to point us to the death of Jesus. In the first Passover, the lambs were sacrificed, and the blood spread on the doorposts so the people could live. But now, the sign is pointing right to Jesus to tell us that, 'The Lamb of God', was also given and his blood spilled so we could have life.

It's curious that the same **place** where the ram died so that Isaac could live was also Mount Moriah (We saw this earlier in this book.) This place was the **very same place** where Jesus was sacrificed so that we could live. This enables us to 'see the meaning' of His death by pointing to the place. In other words – just like Abraham loved his only son, God shows us His love for us through Father Love and the love of His only Son. We remember this in connection with the **place** that this occurred.

So, in two different ways (through **timing** and through **place**) two of the most symbolic and significant events in the Old Testament are signs pointing directly to the death of Jesus. I cannot think of any other person in history whose death is so foreshadowed by two parallels in such a dramatic fashion. Can you?

"Christ our Passover has been sacrificed for us." 1 Corinthians. 5:7

There are three things to take notice of:

1. God said the Angel of Death would pass through Egypt and strike down the firstborn, both: men and animals. He did not say that it would only be the Egyptians. No, He would strike down anyone who was not protected by the blood.

2. God did not come at that time to judge those struck down. He said He would bring judgment on the *gods* of Egypt. Not the people. His judicial authority will come at the Final Judgment.

3. This was a striking on Egypt (representing the world), not just the Egyptians. So anyone living in Egypt, the Pharaoh, the Egyptians, the Israelites and the animals were in harm's way.

Essentially this striking down of Egypt, pictorially, was declaring that in the future God in Christ would come to strike down our bondage to the world.

This is the 10th plague (also known as the Plague of the Firstborn) and throughout history, it has been celebrated as the Feast of Passover — but did this event actually take place? Up until now all of this has been the forewarning. The Lord has an uncanny way of stating what will happen. He will then follow that up by showing us in scripture that the actual event does, in fact, take place just as it was described and in the same detail and sequence. And as we read we get to watch it unfold as it is painted out in Scripture.

We end this week with the climax of the story:

As you are waiting to see what the imposing fate of Egypt will be, remember that you have walked through the door and are inside the protective covering of the blood stained doorposts. You, however, are privy to this grand information and facts from an entirely different vantage point than Moses or the people of Israel. They were unaware of the outcome. These frightful events have not taken place for them at this point! In their frame of reference, this has only been a warning phase.

Please read Exodus 12:21-30:

What did Moses do? What did he say to the people (use your own words)?

_____

_____

What did the people do in **verse 27b & 28**?

_____

They prepared. And one of the integral parts to the preparation was their reverence. Beautiful reverence was their response and then they each 'could' do 'just' what the Lord commanded! God is faithful! He will let nothing come between Himself and His people. We see the completion. At midnight...

Read verse 29. Who was struck down first?

_____

I know that this answer is sometimes a difficult one to comprehend with a lens of love. But if you put on the True Love lens and then view it again you can see that the one who puts themselves in charge of making the decisions is always the most accountable for their actions. What Pharaoh decreed in **Exodus 1:22** became his own appointment (refer to the fourth day of this week).

I want to scrape your chin up off the floor. The Lord is completely just and loving. Can you identify with His Father Heart of Love? It may be a bit unique to ask you this right here. How we view God, and His character has everything to do with how we view Him. Is this through the lens of love or fear? If He doesn't compromise on all that He promised in keeping the covenant, then this should be a security to you. The blood is the significance of the covenant. God the Father, in Jesus, in complete oneness, gave His own life in His full love so that you could be saved.

This was the only **actual** Pass-over. This Pass-over was the only time this took place in this way; all the other Passover celebrations were to remember this particular event. The only exception was the day in which Jesus fulfilled the Passover Feast with Himself on the cross at just the right **time** in just the right **place**.

To make way for our deliverance out of bondage from 'Egypt' — the Lamb was slain. The blood was shed. God appointed and accepted the sacrifice of the Lamb. We see that this particular Pass-over was the herald for the future that would take place on Calvary. In the fullness of atonement, God would pass over giving us forgiveness and life. Jesus only through Jesus!

Do you feel involved in the story now?

Just as the spilled blood of the lamb completely covered the doorpost securing the life of all those who were appropriated in it, Jesus is the Lamb slain from the foundations of the world.

The Precious Blood of Jesus!!

Next Week

We continue to study the lasting impact Passover has had for all eternity. Brace yourself the force draws you to God. You won't want to miss it!

Week 5

Royalty & Righteousness

Last week

We had a journey back in time, didn't we? As a quick review, we took a look at the life of Joseph and how through him the Israelites moved to Egypt. Then we saw that after Joseph had died a new Pharaoh came to power. He forced them to work under heavy labor, and he established an edict that each firstborn son was to be killed, and this was the period in history when Moses was born. It was a miracle from God that he lived. During his life, Moses attempted to obey God. One of the ways he did this was by asking Pharaoh to let the Israelite people go so they could worship God in the desert. Each time Pharaoh refused to release them a different plague hit Egypt.

We studied the worst one, the Plague of the Firstborn - also known as Passover, it did, however, have a way out for the Israelites. But, **each** member of the family was responsible for taking the provision for himself. We saw that the 'blood' and the 'door' have far-reaching meaning and symbolism. Didn't you delight in understanding this?

This week

As we continue to study the lasting impact Passover has had for all eternity, I want us to think about something. What we are learning holds so much meaning. But our understanding needs to be opened. We want to realize that what God did and said in the Old Testament is the background He intends for us to have to understand the New Testament. We often come to God's climactic words and read right over them because we have not followed the inherent drama that would reveal the true richness. To fully experience the thrust and impact of what God is saying to us, we are going to continue with the storyline that led to the Israelites massive exodus from Egypt. This included some irritating grumbling in the desert and the intensity of Moses receiving the covenant of the Law. Brace yourself this dramatic force does draw you to God.

So, come, draw near.

As you yearn and learn to draw close to God, this is His promise to you –

"Draw near to God and He will draw near to you." James 4:8

So how do you draw near to God?

Good question. He is always with you. He says to seek Him.

"You will seek me and find me when you seek me with all your heart. I will be found by you, declares the Lord." Jeremiah 29: 13 & 14a

What a thought provoking challenge. God promises to be found. You just have to seek. In other words, be earnest hungering and thirsting, craving God Himself. Not just the things of God, but God. His presence. His company. His companionship. His love. His faithfulness. Him. Just to be with Him. The point is, God is crazy about you. His love for you is beyond that of anyone ever. He wants you to recognize and identify His True Love. To put it another way, that you would feel His love for you.

And not surprising, since we are talking about covenant (a two-sided relationship), God wants to be loved too. For you to be crazy about Him. So go ahead it is OK to open up your heart and let your love pour out from the deep depths of your soul. He can't hear you love upon Him enough, not because He needs to hear you. It is because He truly desires intimacy with you.

Let's define covenant:

What aspects of covenant have you learned over the last few weeks? **Write down** one that just stands out to you.

_____

_____

First

We are in this great epic adventure in the wilderness with Pharaoh, Moses, and the Israelites and of course God. We are here because of our desire to know God's passionate love for us that warrants delving into the material we ordinarily summarize in church or other study groups and are therefore not necessarily able to catch the full significance.

We pick up where the Angel of Death struck down the firstborn sons in Egypt. There was more wailing at that moment than ever before or ever since as not one house in Egypt (that was not covered by the blood) was without someone dead. Wow! Cataclysmic! Pharaoh was outraged.

The Mass Exodus:

Please read Exodus 12:31-39:

What did Pharaoh tell Moses and Aaron to do in **verse 31**?

_____

What did the Egyptians urge the Israelites to do and why in **verse 33**?

_____

What did the Israelites ask the Egyptians for in **verses 35 & 36**?

_____

Remember from last week that this was foretold as a promise of God in Exodus 3:22.
"And I will make the Egyptians favorably disposed toward this people, so that when you leave you will not go empty-handed."

      So the Israelites plundered the Egyptians. <u>God's provision for the desert times!</u>

How many people were there in **Exodus 12:37**?

_____

Who else accompanied the Israelites in **verse 38**?

_____

The 'many others' could have been the Egyptians of Exodus 9:20.
"Those officials of Pharaoh who feared the word of the Lord hurried to bring their slaves and their livestock inside."

The life-saving blood was for **each** person who applied it to the doorposts. Anyone who had the blood was spared, this would include any God fearing obedient Egyptian as well. If I were an Egyptian and I was a witness to those horrific plagues, I would have watched to see what the Israelites were doing and followed them very carefully doing exactly what they did. Wouldn't you? They were being spared from what I was enduring - God was protecting them, and I would have wanted to be protected also.

Incredible! Realize that the Israelites had been set free from Egypt and Pharaoh after more than 400 years of captivity. Think about that for a minute. Our country has only been around for just over 200 years - that's twice as long. Free! Now they were free. Right? Free to do what and go where?

So where was Moses headed with God's people? To the 'Promised Land'. **Right?**

Remember God's words to Pharaoh, **"Let my people go, so that they may worship me in the desert."** They had the glorious opportunity of worshiping and meeting the Promiser. However, if they went straight to the Promised Land without having a revelation of God they would end up desiring to go back to their old way of life in Egypt. Israel's deliverance from Egyptian bondage correlates to our deliverance from the slavery of sin and the world. Egypt is a type of world system, and the Israelites a type of the church. Once the Lord has led us out of our Egypt (our bondage to sin and death) and made us a new creation in Christ, He wants to be sure we have had a revelation of Him, His presence. This way we won't get frustrated or bored and quickly return to our old ways and habits.

Please look up Exodus 3:3- 4:

We have already seen this scripture in one of our earlier sections but go back to these two verses with me to see something you may not have observed the first time. Before we go any further though, please note that this revelation of God, took place at Mount Sinai, which was called Horeb, the Mountain of God. The same Mount Sinai we are going to get acquainted with this week.

Read these verses carefully and thoughtfully. Do you see it? When does God draw near to Moses?

Write out verse 4 below:

_____

_____

It was not until Moses had gone over to look (or in different words, to draw near to the Lord's presence) that anything happened between the Lord and Moses. It was at the moment when God had Moses' see his own true intentions that God revealed Himself and spoke. When we draw near to God He will draw close enough for us to realize Him.

God showed Moses a part of Himself - His heart. Meeting God there for the first time at Mount Sinai unquestionably changed Moses. Can you imagine? Because if he had not seen and heard from God in that burning bush, Moses' intentions could have been different. But **now** his heart was with God's Heart, to deliver God's people. He couldn't stop short. Because of Moses, the Israelites would become beneficiaries of seeing and hearing and drawing near to God with a greater intimate knowledge of Him.

God led Moses and His people out into the desert to worship. To a quiet place of rest?...?

We return to our story… Please read Exodus 13:17-18. Write this below in your own words as you see that God has no shortcuts:

_____

We usually cannot take the short road or the shortcuts in life. The easy way out is not always the best for us. If we have life either too easy or too hard, we may return to Egypt—the world. God knows what is best. He knows that He is best for us. His leading. So He goes with us everywhere (or better put we go with Him everywhere). How did this look for the Israelites in **Exodus 13:21-22**?

By day _____   By night _____

Notice in **verse 22** the word **left**. God never left them. He loves His covenant people!

Was His presence in front of them or behind them? _____

God knew they would need Him again because Pharaoh would be in hot pursuit of them immediately.

Something is about to happen...

Continue as you read Exodus 14:5-14:

Sure enough, Pharaoh changed his mind. He wanted to have his free labor back (brick and mortar laying). Pharaoh pursued the Israelites, and they were terrified and cried out to the Lord. Notice that they didn't commune with God directly. They couldn't. They had not had a personal revelation of God yet. So they had to go through Moses. They grumbled. It was constant and continuous grumbling and complaining to their leader. Fear had led them to want to return to Egypt because they thought death was feasible in the desert (verses 11-12).

Moses response in **verse 13** was?

_____

It is interesting that Moses told all of them to stand firm and be still.

Look closely at the surety of Moses. He promised them something from God. He promised them deliverance. Reflect on how God has been faithful to His promise to deliver you? Have you ever been desperate? Notice what the Lord did for the desperate Israelites. Be prepared to see the wonder of God!

Please read Exodus 14:15-28:

Here are a few highlights of this astonishing act of God:

1. It was the staff and **faith** in God that were used to divide the water.
2. The Israelites walked on dry ground.
3. The angel of the Lord, who had been with them in the cloud and fire, withdrew and went **behind** them as a shield and defender.
4. A wall of water - piled up. Visualize this. Can you?
5. God made the wheels of their chariots come off - this is so like God to think so practically.
6. After Moses had stretched out his hand, the waters engulfed the Egyptians. Just as God had promised through Moses in Exodus 14:13, not one of Pharaoh's people survived, so they never had to see them again.

   Complete victory!

Their original journey in the desert took a little over 3 months. During this time the Israelites got to see the marvelous glory of God! The pure revelation of His power and might! Water from a rock - bitter to sweet. Manna and quail for food. The battle with the Amalekites that they won because Moses kept his hands lifted high to God with the help of his friends. All these signs and wonders and yet they grumbled and complained and constantly wanted to go back to Egypt. Go back to the 'world'. How we do this too. We get a meaningful and clear view of God and yet we grumble. Especially in our desperate times. We cling to the world and many of its ways instead of pressing on to win the prize of knowing Christ Jesus our Lord.

Second

Three months later, Moses and the Israelites arrived and camped at the foot of Mount Sinai, the Mountain of God (the approximate location of the burning bush). Moses left the people and climbed up to be in the manifest presence of God. God had a message for Moses to give to **every** man, woman, and child who had been delivered out of Egypt.

Please read Exodus 19:1-6:

A surprising message from God!!

Fill in the blanks of verses 4 & 5:

"You yourselves have _____ what I did to Egypt, and how I _____ you on eagles wings and brought you to_____. Now ____ you obey me _____ and keep my _____ then out of all the nations you will be my treasured possession."

That word **IF** really throws a punch doesn't it? Not only the word **IF** but also the word **FULLY**. They had to obey God fully and keep His covenant, then and only then would they be God's treasured possession. But, I thought God cut covenant with Himself to establish a two-sided relationship? Why so many stipulations all of a sudden?

Let's pause. Please glance at this with me for a moment— right here, right in this conditional moment. God tells us the whole reason we were created. **God wants to bring us to Himself!** Wow!! I can hardly breathe. This same God that led them everywhere by His power and might wanted them. He wants me, and He wants you. He truly wants you, did you hear that? Sometimes it is hard to hear it. Sometimes we feel unworthy, or maybe we are too critical of ourselves to be able to comprehend this blessing. But, oh yes the glory of God's love is true.

God leads us out of bondage and doesn't just leave us 'there' alone, He gives us Himself: (read this again)

God wants to dwell with us (He is in us)!! To bring us to Himself!!

Before we move on in Exodus please read 1Peter 2:4-5 (keep bookmarked):

We as New Covenant believers are being built into what? _____ _____

To be a what? _____ _____

Now go back to reading Exodus 19:5b & 6. Fill in the blanks:

"**Although the whole earth is mine, you will be for me a kingdom of _____ and a holy nation. These are the _____ you are to _____ to the Israelites.**"

In the New Testament Peter links our role as God's dwelling place (a spiritual house) with the priesthood.

Back in the Old Testament, only priests could come close to God without judgment. The definition of a priest is someone who can come near to God to minister to Him. They took care of His 'Holy Things' in the Tabernacle (this was future and not yet fully revealed at this point in history in Exodus 19). It would be the Levites that were chosen by God to be the priests. (We see this with Aaron's rod that budded from a dry stick - God did the choosing -- Aaron was a Levite – (Numbers 17))

So to come close to God, you had to be a priest.

Now please read 1Peter 2:9. Fill in the blanks below:

"**But you are a _____ people, a _____ _____, a holy nation, a people belonging to God, that you may declare the_____ of him who called you out of darkness into his wonderful light.**"

We are that royal priesthood - that holy nation. In order to minister to Him, we must be **Royal Priests**. We are royalty! God is our King. He is pure royalty. Only royalty can fellowship with royalty. We must be priests (remember only the priests could come close to God and minister to Him). This would become a new order of priests after Jesus' death and resurrection.

I hope you are starting to truly comprehend this!

Go back to Exodus 19:5b:

As you relate these verses together note that the words of **1Peter 2:9** were originally spoken by God to the people of Israel. He spoke this to **every** one of them just as He speaks this to **every** one of us.

They had been delivered out from Egypt, and now God wanted to get the Egypt out of them. Be holy! For the Lord to dwell in us, He says, "Get the world out of you." This is known as sanctification. Please note that we are completely spotless and holy when we receive the righteousness of Christ, but there is a process for our habits, emotions, and attitudes to align with that reality.

So Moses was told to consecrate the people.

Read Exodus 19:10 -11:

They were to rid themselves of the filth of Egypt.

Look up the word <u>consecrate</u> in your dictionary and write the definition below:

_____

_____

What does this consecration look like for us in the New Covenant?

Imagine this with me:

Two people are standing facing each other. One is wearing a pitch black coat, the other adorned in a pearly white coat. Because of our sin nature, which we were all born into due to Adam's sin, we are the ones wearing the black coat. Picture, with me, that you are clothed in this heavy, filthy dirty, stained, grotesque black coat. This black coat represents your sin. You are standing there face to face with your soon to be Covenant Partner who is robed in the most brilliant, vivid, pure shiny white coat that you have ever seen.

He looks at you with such eyes of **love**. He asks you for your coat. You really can't believe your ears. Why would He want your filthy coat? You unbutton it, pull it off, and start to hand it to Him when all of a sudden He reaches in and quickly places His white coat of righteousness on every part of your being. Now what happened in this exchange is that He first put on Himself - your black coat, bearing all of your sin debt in full because this had to take place before the coat of righteousness could be situated so perfectly on you. It seems simultaneous, but He had to first pay a great price to take your coat. He had to go to the cross wearing your filthy coat and give His life, His blood.

As you stand before Him mesmerized in your new, spotless, blameless, righteous beauty, you realize, just a fraction of what kind of **love** this must require.

You are both standing there face to face when you comprehend that you are now wearing something that can never be stripped or taken away from you. Clothed forever in this covering of righteousness. Incredible! And almost unbelievable!

Now in this surreal moment, I want to add a bit of humor – wouldn't you agree with me that we are sometimes critical of ourselves and also of others? Because of that which we can only perceive with our eyes, we still see parts of the old filthy black coat. So we sometimes fixate on the dark spots that seem to appear here and there on our white coat. We see ourselves and each other as cows. Cows are white right, with black spots? We obsess on our current sins when God has made us white as snow – and this is how He will always see us. (Yes, we do still sin, that is our flesh or the black spots, but our sins have been completely forgiven, so in actuality, they are not really there.)

We must **see** ourselves as the righteousness of Christ. So from now on continuously recall that beautiful white coat and what it cost Jesus to give it to you. Amazing Love!!

God wants you to know that He **TOTALLY** loves you. What will it take for you to be fully persuaded of His love for you? No power or circumstance can take away His love because the cross was sufficient. Jesus's blood was enough. There is nothing more certain than that God loves you. You cannot walk with God and not be impacted and changed by His love. He is saying to you.... "Receive My love.... Bask in My love.... Walk in My love.... I am Love." He keeps us by His love.....

God was going to make an appearance to the people at the base of Mount Sinai.

Go back now to Exodus 19:10-12 and read this carefully:

His appearance is full of majesty and they would have to be ready for Him, consecrated holy. Remember they were sent to the desert to worship God. Was this an inward or an outward preparation?

_____

What were the limits that were set around the mountain? And why?

_____

We put this all together now:

Remember one of our questions at the beginning of this week was, "How do we draw near to God?" Moses found out how. It started when God appeared to him in that burning bush. Moses drew closer to look. He inquired more about the incredible wonder of God. The moment Moses drew near, God called to him.

There was an intimacy that transpired as God called, "Moses," and Moses answered, "Here I am." But God stopped Moses -

> **"You must consecrate yourself. You must take off your sandals because I am holy and the place where I dwell is holy ground." Exodus 3:5**

Moses had to have reverence he had to be holy. Separate from the world. God desired the Israelites to be His treasured possession, a kingdom of priests and a holy nation. God's foreshadowing — He was going to create a royal priesthood. Remember this would be the priests who minister to the **heart** of God. His people would be built into a spiritual house and be royal priests.

Visualize yourself wearing your white coat of righteousness:

This is how you are made holy, spotless and blameless — Jesus' righteousness. The coat of a royal priest. You have been given the privilege of taking care of God's 'Holy Things' (ministering to the heart of God). We worship God to give glory and honor and praise to the One who is worthy. We must give Him our whole heart the inside and the outside. Leaving behind the world and being washed by Jesus' blood. We become a habitation for God to dwell. So take a moment to take a closer look. Inquire more about the incredible wonder of God.

The Israelites were released from bondage to go and worship God in the desert. Material provisions were given to them in advance. They traveled 3 months in pursuit of the Promised Land. God went with them and never left them in the day or the night. He was in front leading the way. When they needed special help as Pharaoh and the Egyptian army marched in to pursue and take them captive again, God then became their rear guard, their shield, and defender. All this because He was in covenant with them. What beautiful faithfulness!

God is in covenant with you. He has released you from the bondage of your 'Egypt.' He has given you the provision you need to face whatever strongholds or baggage you have, and to 'deal' with them, and then to let them go. Remember He has promised you abundant life - 'the Promised Land.'

Key: You can **not** have abundant life and still be thinking about returning to 'Egypt' (the world and all of its ways). God wants you free, so you can enjoy worshiping Him even in the desert times. Yes, it's true, I have seen this in my own life. There will be a depth to your release from self-loathing, your prideful dignity and your need of acceptance from people. **How you claim God's promise** liberates you from perfectionism, shame, anger, unforgiveness, depression, addiction or whatever causes you to grumble in the desert. In your life here and now He has vowed to you—the 'Promised Land'. There **is** a life of freedom and rest. It is found in HIM. God goes with you day and night. He is leading your way. He is your shield and defender against your enemy. This is covenant.

Third

Look at God's impressive appearance. Everyone trembled!

Please read Exodus 19:16-25:

The very same people who had seen God's delivering power had never seen His revealed glory. As He started revealing His glory they drew back. Smoke and fire billowed up. The whole mountain trembled violently. The sound of the trumpet grew louder and louder.

Where did the Lord descend to in **verse 20**?_____

In what form in **verse 18**?_____

Who did He call to join Him in **verse 20**?_____

The Israelites **drew back.** Moses was called to **draw near**.

God gave Moses strict instructions on how they were to approach Him. What would happen if they did not obey?

_____

What did God say to Moses about the priests in **verse 22**?

_____

No one could go up to His manifest presence because He had put limits around the mountain and set it apart as holy. Consider why at that time only Moses and not even the priests could approach God.

God sent Moses back down the mountain. Then God spoke these words ...

Read Exodus 20:1:
What do you think it means here that 'God spoke these words'?

_____

Never in all of history has there ever been such a sermon preached. The preacher was God Himself. This was a Law of His own making, a Law of His own speaking. God never spoke at any time or at any occasion since the Fall in the Garden of Eden, as He spoke the Ten Commandments . The Law had been given to man in the Garden of Eden - it was written in their hearts. But, sin so marred the knowledge of it that God had to revive it in this new manner.

Let's assess the reason for the Law. What is going on here? I thought God 'cut' covenant with Himself creating the Abrahamic Covenant, so why the Law? Why this new covenant? If salvation is by faith, and Abraham was saved by faith, apart from the Law, then why the Law?

Take note of the order of these two covenants. **Circle the one that came first:**

        The Law   Abrahamic Covenant

Since the Law came after the Abrahamic Covenant, does this mean that the Law replaced or altered the Abrahamic Covenant? _____

Think about it, God heard the Israelites cry for help when they were under heavy labor in Egypt. He remembered His covenant with Abraham. Think with me of the word covenant. Now that you are learning more about it, you're growing to understand the depth of this word. God **remembered** His covenant; this captures so much meaning in just one single word. God keeps His promises. He pledged to give His life, love, and protection forever in the most sacred of bonds. He remembered His covenant, so why was it that the first thing He did after He freed them from captivity was to give them the Law?

Look up Galatians 3:15-18 (and bookmark). In your own words describe what Paul is saying:

_____
_____

When a covenant has been established can it be set aside or added to according to **verse 15**? _____
In **verse 16** who does it say is the Seed? _____

This Law that God was about to give the Israelites was 430 years after He gave them the Covenant of His promise in blood with Abraham. Does this new Law set that covenant aside? _____

81

What does the inheritance depend on in **verse 18**? _____

How wonderful is this? The inheritance doesn't depend on keeping anything, especially this Law that God now required of the Israelites. We need to try to understand God here. We are speaking of inheritance, the promise of God.

The **Law** was something **you keep,** and a **promise** is something **you claim**.

We all get to claim the promise of the Covenant. Why was the Law needed? Let's find out together.

Continue reading in Galatians 3:19:

What does it say was the reason for the Law?

_____

The Law was given to define transgressions, to define sin, to explain to man what sin is.

> **"I would not have known what sin was except through the law. For I would not have known what coveting really was if the law had not said, 'Do not covet'." Romans 7:7**

Paul's point here is that the Law was simply added. It did not replace the Abrahamic Covenant. It was added **until** the Seed (Jesus) could come. **He has come!!** But for the Israelites this was only something they were told would take place in the future. At that time they could claim the promise of God and be saved by faith, just like Abraham.

Both covenants were given by God. The Law does not contradict the need for the Seed. The Law does not keep a man righteous. If the Law could keep a man righteous then Jesus died for nothing! And if that was true then we could just keep a bunch of rules and be deemed good enough to go to heaven. This is the 'works theology'. That doesn't work. Christ is our only answer.

> **"All have sinned and fall short of the glory of God." Romans 3:23**

The Israelites had broken their part of the covenant with God. Remember the **IF** you obey me **FULLY** part from earlier this week? God was about to convey to the Israelites just what His standard is and how far short they all came because of their transgressions – rebellion (not worship) in the desert to God.

The Law reveals man as a sinner in need of a Savior.

Let me give you an analogy:

In your bathroom, you probably have a mirror over your sink. This mirror is a picture of the Law. You do not wash with the mirror; it only reveals the dirt. So it is with the Law, it reveals sin. It shows the sinful condition. You can look in the mirror and think you look alright. Likewise, you may believe you are following the Lord.

But the Law does not lie. Neither does the mirror. The fault is not in the mirror. The mirror, like the Law, does not make you clean. (Only the blood can make you clean)

Below explain in your own words the reason for the Law:

_____

_____

Man's need to cover up...

Fourth

Man's need to try and cover up was Adam and Eve's first response when they disobeyed God's Law in the Garden (do not eat from the tree of the knowledge of good and evil). Ever since that fateful moment, humanity was destined to live in shame with an inherent need to self-protect, by self-effort.

The basis of the Law has been around since before time began it is God's Law.

I give you some insight:

1. The Law is a revelation of God, of Who He Is. Through it, we can see a part of His wonder and His perfection and power. The Law in itself cannot enforce itself. The Law-giver enforces it, the One with all the power.

2. The Law is an expression of the holy will of God. It is not a vague notion or something we do with good intentions. No, the Law requires perfection on man's part. It necessitates perfect obedience because the Law of the Lord is perfect.

"So then, the law is holy, and the commandment is holy, righteous and good." Romans 7: 12

3. The Law is right. We are fallen beings living in a fallen world colored by our environment, so we do not know what is right or wrong. Through the Law, God shows the line between good and evil.

4. There is no love in the Law. There is no grace in the Law. The Law gives heed to what man ought to be. Love and grace show off who God is.

5. The Law was given to lead man to **Christ**.

There is only one way to salvation for both the Jew and the Gentile, (Israelite and us) faith in a Savior. In Christ, the Law was not given as a means of salvation. No, it was given as a way for us to see our need for salvation and thus a Savior.

Let's go over this from a different angle...

Please read Romans 4:1-3:

What does it say that Abraham was **not** justified by in **verse 2**?_____

Why? _____

Abraham believed God and it was credited to him as what? _____

Continue reading now in Romans 4:9-12:

Under what circumstance was righteousness credited to him before or after he was circumcised in **verse 10**?
Circle the correct answer:

Before   After

In **verse 11** when did he receive the sign or the seal of this righteousness, when he was?
Circle the correct answer:

Circumcised   Uncircumcised

Who is Abraham father to in **verse 11 & 12**? **Explain:**

_____

Continuing in Romans 4:13:
It was not through the Law that Abraham and his offspring received the promise. What was it through?

_____

Fill in the blanks of Romans 4:14 & 16:

"For if those who live by _____are heirs, faith has ___ value and the promise is worthless, because law brings _____. And where there is no law there is no transgression. Therefore, the _____ comes by faith, so that it may be by _____ and may be guaranteed to all Abraham's offspring."

What does the Law bring? _____
What does faith bring? _____

Are you getting this yet?

Faith, belief, and trust in God are what bring the promise. It is wholly by grace. The Law can actually stimulate sin if our eyes are continuously focused on our human fleshly need to try and make ourselves right with God.

We are almost finished viewing this from enough angles but... **the next part is crucial!**

Please read Hebrews 8:8-11:

Where does it say God will put His Law in **verse 10**?
In their _____
and write it on their _____

I love the last part of **verse 11** it says that they will know the Lord, **KNOW** Him. God still desires above all else to be our God and for us to be His people. If the Law is in our minds and written on our hearts, His Spirit living in us will cause us to know Him. Know His heart.

One last a bit of insight read 2 Corinthians 3:2-6:

We have been referred to in these verses as a letter from Christ. Was that letter written with ink or by the Spirit of the living God?

_____

Was it written on tablets of stone or on tablets of human hearts?

_____

Notice it says that God has made us competent as ministers of a New Covenant - we are ministers which mean priests.

Exodus 31:18:

"When the Lord finished speaking to Moses on Mount Sinai, he gave him the two tablets of the testimony, the tablets of stone inscribed by the finger of God."

There are two things I want to bring to your attention:

1. The Old Covenant of the Law was written by the finger of God or in other words by His miraculous power. Do you think that the New Covenant, the letter written by the Spirit of the living God, was also written by the finger of God on our hearts? Why or why not?

   _____

2. Notice that there were two stone tablets. Why do you think two were needed?

   _____

Let's summarize:

First of all, it is fascinating to see the completeness of God's plan. There were two tablets of stone, not in case one smashed and broke or because half of the Ten Commandments where on one side and half on the other side as we so often see depicted. It was the practice of covenant making to establish duplicate documents. One was made for each party of the covenant, one for Israel and one for God.

Remember this was God's covenant, so all the stipulations of the covenant were His. He wrote them by His power. The power, remember, to enforce the Law comes from the Law-giver. We are a letter from Christ, and as such, the Spirit of the living God has written His Law upon our hearts and put it in our minds. We have the capacity to obey these laws in an entirely different way than the Israelites. We have that same power that wrote the Law and enforces the Law living on the inside of us. Do you see this? That power, the power of God to enforce the Law, lives in you and me. We are not under the Law, but we are empowered by the Holy Spirit to live out this Law by His grace. Amazing grace! Amazing God!

We live on the New Covenant side of the **until** (the Seed came). Christ died just as the Scriptures foretold and rose to conquer death, ascended to the right hand of the Father and He sent the Holy Spirit to live in us.

Circumcision, the sign of the covenant, is now a matter of the heart!!

1. The Abrahamic Covenant (although it included obligations) — **stressed God's promise**.
2. The Mosaic Law — **stressed human responsibility**.

Now the question comes up. Are you fully persuaded about all of this?

Fifth

This great exchange took place for me 25 plus years ago on a chaise chair in my back yard while working on my homework for a women's study on the book of Hebrews. I was learning, but things were still considerably unclear to me. The study culminated to these verses in Hebrews.

"For the word of God is living and active. Sharper than any double-edged sword, it penetrates even to dividing soul and spirit, joints and marrow; it judges the thoughts and attitudes of the heart. Nothing in all creation is hidden from God's sight. Everything is uncovered and laid bare before the eyes of him to whom we must give account." Hebrews 4:12-13.

Busted!! Not only could God know my thoughts and judge my motives but all I had ever done good or bad would be displayed before His vast eyes of knowledge. Yikes!

I had a sorted past, to say the least. I was 29 at the time looking to find love but in all the wrong places. Alcohol, drugs, low self-esteem, yearnings for more worldly lusts, they all had such a pull on me.

*That day in my backyard something clicked. I just wanted to be good. I had always truly wanted this my whole life. However, I had been running in the wrong direction confused and lost. But, that day, I met **A** heart like no other. I met the Lord's, heart. He is beyond incredible. I knew He was what I had truly been searching for with such a passion, but had been elusive to find up until that moment.*

*When I think about it now it is interesting to me that to the depth of my driven passion for the wrong things, I now have, to that same intensity, a driven passion for the Lord and His beautiful heart of **love**.*

*As I shared with you in a previous section, God has been working to rid me of this undercurrent of self-loathing. He has asked me to lay down one Isaac after the other. As this has occurred, pain has inevitably ensued. The years have trickled by as God has been encouraging me to believe, ever more strongly, what I asked you at the end of the fourth section. **Am I fully persuaded of His love for me?***

I was standing with my co-worker Tom Bradburn in the chapel at a church in North Phoenix when I received a cell phone call from my dad. He sounded dismayed, so I stepped out into the ladies room. His next words were words no daughter wants to ever hear from the dad they love, "I have pancreatic cancer." I listened to the details with my little heart in shock.

It was only three years earlier that I had heard the words from my dad, "Your mom as had a brain aneurysm and they have air vac her to the hospital, they are not sure if she will even make the helicopter flight in". I received those words at a Target, where I left my cart, and rushed to my car, dazed. We never know when a crisis will come knocking at our door. We may even think we are above it all and that circumstances like this happen to others, 'not me or my family'. In fact, we may even doubt God's love if we perceive that He is having or letting us go through it. Have you ever felt like this? God, do you really love me or not? Why are you putting me through this? I remember boarding the airplane back then wondering the whole time what I would encounter. Seeing your mom with all those tubes and life support puts a new appreciation in your heart of the love you have for someone, no matter how strained the relationship may have been. The look in my dad's eyes that day was one of 'how can I ever live without her.' After surviving excruciating trauma, followed by a tremendous effort on my mom's part, she made, literally, a miraculous recovery.

So upon hearing my dad's words from my cell phone that day, I returned to the chapel with a similar fear and dread. I must have had the appearance that portrayed it all because one person asked me "Who died." A bad choice of words as I explained what I had just learned. Eric Scroggins, whom I had only met about 15 minutes prior to the call, took both Tom's and my hands and launched out into prayer for my dad, me, my family and my nerves that were shot at that point. I had been a Christian for a long time by then and had prayed with many people and in a significant number of groups but that day, wow that day, that prayer was different. Fervent and piercing straight to the core of God's compassion. When he said "Amen", I just sat there paralyzed with emotion. Not exactly sure where all the emotion had welled up from, of course for my dad, but there was more to it. I looked at Tom, was he also aware of the Lord's weighty presence to that intensity at that moment. Yes, indeed the expression on his face made that evident.

Reaching out with all of my energy I thanked Eric, then I asked him, "Where did you learn to pray like that and how do you have such confidence? You were not worried what anyone, even someone you just met, would think of your zeal, eagerness, empathy, and love." You see I struggled, as many of you may as well, with fear of what others might think of me. I fretted about each different encounter I had with individual people and even more so when I was in a group. Overtaking me with the fear of repercussions, backlash, and rejection. Fear of rejection has been such a debilitating challenge for me.

Eric's answer to me changed my life…..

*He stated, "When you are fully persuaded of God's **love** for you, you will no longer care what others think or say about you. You will live **free**!"*

*I asked, "But how do I grasp that kind of **love** – fully persuaded?"*

*He replied, **"You will know when you know."***

That day I asked the Lord to show me this **love**. I never envisioned I would discover a blessing through situations I never imagined would happen to me. (I will be unfolding this in context with covenant over the next two weeks. I am eager to share it with you.)

Next week

We journey to the top. Just as Moses was invited to come up the mountain to be in God's presence, He invites us to come to the top to be with Him as well. Come up higher!!

Week 6

The Top

Last week

We studied some of the dramatic storylines that led up to one of God's covenants, the covenant of the Law. We noticed why God did not have Moses lead the Israelites straight into the Promised Land. The Lord first accompanied them into the desert so they could have a revelation of His glory. His great desire, then and now, is to dwell with us - not just visit. The most important thing we determined is that God's desire is to bring us to Himself. For each one of us individually. What an amazingly personal God He is. Out there in the desert, the Israelites were promised His presence, by day the Pillar of Cloud and by night the Pillar of Fire. Unfortunately, it was clearly revealed that the Israelites response to God was to run away, to desire to turn back to Egypt ('the world').

We concentrated our attention on why and how God sent forth an added covenant. Remember that Moses came down from the mountain and God spoke words that would add an understanding and a sense of just how holy the Lord is and how we come short of His perfect standard. And the number one aim was to show us our need for a Savior. The Law did not replace the Abrahamic Covenant it was simply added. For the Israelite, the Law was something you kept, and the promise of the Abrahamic Covenant was something you claimed.

This week

We will see the close proximity between our level of determination and our level of intimacy with God. What do we desire to have with Him? Moses was invited to come up the mountain to be in God's presence. The Lord also invites us to come to the top to be with Him. God has given us the permission to choose our level of assent and the speed at which we travel. As we journey, we will notice something about our traveling companions.

This week I want to thank you in advance for permitting me to come into your life and share from the seriousness of my life experience. Opening up is hard for many of us, and I am no exception. I do know that during this agonizing time of trial other people's stories helped me immensely. I hope that mine will be that for someone, maybe even you.

We need to see some honest realities of who you and I would be without God. We don't often think we are that bad, do we? Not really, just a tad here and there. But God sets the rules, the laws, and the standard. As a fallen being, we can never be in His presence for one moment, without the blood. The Blood of Jesus Christ fulfills God's 'need' for us to keep the Law. Thank You, God, for Your grace! Spend a few moments exalting the Name of the Lord. Wholeheartedly worship the Lord of glory!!

Let's define covenant:

Below please write out what you think the difference is between the Abrahamic covenant and the Law (Mosaic Covenant).

_____

_____

First

As I bask and soak in the delight of the truth of all I have been sharing with you for the past five weeks, God's unparalleled love is marvelous. Yet I may live as if His love is too good to be true. If I don't fully absorb and nurture the truth of this intense True Love, I may still rely on my own strength for the things that come up in my life and try to control these areas of concern on my own.

I want to ask you a very poignant question. Sincerely, what do you think of God's **love** now? After learning what He planned, orchestrated, established, suffered, and secured for you, what do you 'see' of His love for you?

Covenant is a huge deal, isn't it? Where has this been all of your life? If you had only known you could have stopped running, seeking, striving alone out there and spun an 180 degree about face and run directly into the arms of the One, who loves you that much. So what might be holding you back from more passionately abandoning yourself and enthusiastically embracing God's love and thus fervently living this New Covenant of life that is truly life?

Look up John 14:6-7. Write out what Jesus says about Himself below:

_____

_____

Jesus is the way the truth and the life. He is life. He is life that is truly life. He is also the way, the only way if you want to have this life that is truly life. Jesus is truth, so if we haven't known covenant we haven't really known **all** the truth about His love. The True Love of the Father.

Not knowing about covenant could have a great deal to do with why you may not have fully embraced and held fast to God's love. If you don't know about something then how can you fully submerge yourself into it all the way down into the depths of your being? There is a spot inside of you that can only be filled with real love and only this amazing True Love. Remember we need to know that Someone TOTALLY loves us.

You may be asking me at this moment, "That's all well and good for you, but I don't feel His love. I mean right here, right now, in my life. What do I do when it doesn't look like or feel like He loves me?"

Jesus has done everything through His death on the cross. And just like Abraham, we have to grasp this by faith. But, have you ever just believed something because someone told you so? Maybe, but most often our human nature wants to see and experience it for ourselves. To research, investigate, ask more questions, and inquire enough knowledge and insight as well as have our own encounter, because we don't want to be naive accepting something without being completely sure it's true. Otherwise, we may believe falsely, and it could affect the rest of our life or at least make us look foolish for being 'had.'

Faith goes deep. But anytime we doubt His love we need to go back and remind ourselves of covenant. Keep plumbing the wells because they are inexhaustible. I have no authority to force your mind and heart to receive this with enough gusto to have confidence. But as you ask the Lord to reveal this to you, He can and He will.

Covenant is two sided:

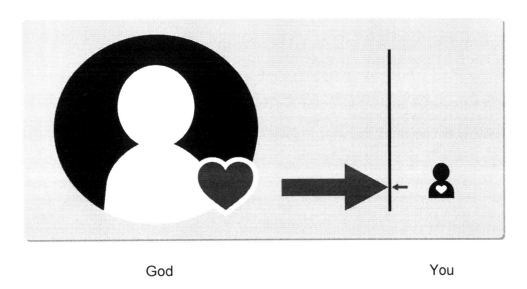

God   You

Please observe this illustration. Of course, you know that I cannot render God as great and immense as He is, but this visual may help a bit. God has done soooo much. He has cut covenant with Himself to secure your position in the most sacred, lasting Covenant of all time. Since covenant is two-sided and you are in this with Him, He is now trying to show you that He has come right up to the edge of that line of His steps toward you. He has come such an unfathomable distance. Love beyond reason, unfailing, everlasting kindness, and attention to every detail. He hasn't missed one thing to show you His love for you. Have you discerned the reality of this yet?

Notice the line in the diagram:
This line is the point up to which God will go. He is gracious, and He will never force Himself on you. Because of partnership, He is saying He has come right up to you doing absolutely everything needed to approach you to have a relationship of intimacy. The next move is yours. And the good news is, He will take your one inch of movement.

We see something as Moses went to get the Law (which included the Ten Commandments). First of all, as you recall God told Moses to get the people consecrated and sanctified, in three days, He was going to come to the base of the mountain. But, God put barriers around the mountain – "don't let them touch it."

Please read Exodus 19:10-12 from last week again as a reminder:

Why do you think God made such a gigantic limitation in **verse 12**?

_____

God was going to come, and where God is must be holy. The Israelites were still too insipid – if they had tangibly touched God's holiness, it would literally have killed them.

In the New Covenant, we can be grateful that we are redeemed to God by the blood of Christ Jesus. In fact, it's hard for many of us to accept this, so we keep trying to 'work' things out with God. In fact, we are probably not going to die if we don't fulfill our side of the relationship (as in performance related aspects). But, we are not going to have the marked degree of intimacy with Him that is accessible. We may miss much of the life that the Lord has for us solely because we have been blocking Him. He won't push, (but He does woo). We want to be able to know the full extent of His love with eyes to see and to be an open vessel to receive.

(In His love) He isn't going to give us what we aren't sincerely ready for – we wouldn't be able to handle it.

God didn't keep the Israelites away from the mountain because He didn't love them. He just didn't want them to get hurt. In our life we may be asking, "But, why couldn't they come close?" If you read further on in Exodus (chapter 32), these are the same people that in Moses' absence quickly pooled together their resources and made a golden calf and bowed down to worshiped it (this from the plunder they got from the Egyptians). Left on their own they became anxious and began to doubt the existence of God, worshiping idols instead. There were, however, a few people who God did include in the journey up...

Please read Exodus 24:1-4:

I would like you to observe this for yourself. Who did the Lord say could come up the mountain besides Moses?

_____
Who was to worship at a distance? _____
Who was to approach? _____
Who was not to go up at all? _____

The only ones allowed to go higher up the mountain than the rest of the Israelite people were the seventy elders, Aaron and Aaron's two sons (the two sons were later struck dead because they chose to offer the wrong fire on the altar of incense).

How would you describe an elder?

_____

Who was Aaron? And why do you think he was included?

_____

Continue reading in Exodus 24:9-11:
They obeyed and ascended the mountain to worship the Lord.

Whom did they see? _____

What was under His feet? _____

Did God allow any harm to come to them? _____

Even though they didn't have the same exact authorization as Moses, they did get to go up higher and see a part of the beauty of God. Only Moses went all the way up to the top, and this because of his depth of relationship.

Aaron would later become the first Levitical priest.

The seventy elders are described in Numbers 11:16 this way, **"The Lord said to Moses: 'Bring me seventy of Israel's elders who are known to you as leaders and officials among the people.'"**

The general mass of the Israelites was restrained to stand around right outside the barrier of the mountain far off from God, or I guess their other option was to worship the golden calf (symbolic of our worship of worldly idols). Again, we saw in the Scripture that the other group got to go up higher and see the beauty of the Lord. But Moses went all the way to the top.

Do you want to go to the top?

In the next section, we will put all of this together........

Second

My heart's greatest desire is to be as tangibly close to the Lord as possible. The Lord is the most wonderful One I have ever known. So how do we soar to the top? And can we consistently stay there?

The seventy elders, Aaron and his two sons got to go a little bit farther up the mountain than the Israelites who were stuck back down at the bottom, waiting. Aaron and the elders must have been extremely excited to see a glimpse of the beauty of the Lord – 'God's feet like on sapphire.' Maybe that was enough for them, after all, they did see something rare. But was that enough? Is that enough for you?

Moses ascended into the cloud to talk to God as a man talks with his friend. (Ex 33:11)

Now, this is different in the New Covenant. The access is open, and all we need to do is focus. God also knows that we determine the level of assent. The degree of intimacy that we desire with Him. **And this is based on our response to receiving God's love.** Have you ever met someone who you detect just has this crazy affection for God? Why does it seem as though some people are closer to Him than others? It is a visible aspect of who they are. There is a reverent familiarity. Talking about the Lord as if indeed they know Him.

In the New Testament of the Bible, we read that there were multitudes that gathered around Jesus to hear Him teach and perform miracles. They were curious enough to look. And just a little closer or higher up the level of 'nearness' to Jesus there were the seventy-two.

Read Luke 10:1-4:
Who did the appointing? _____
Who and how many were appointed? _____
What were they appointed to do? _____

_____

This group of people may have been 70 – other manuscripts use the figure 72. So right out from among the multitude, Jesus appoints elders to be 'workers' sent out into the harvest field. To every town ahead of where He was about to go.

Read Mark 3:13-14:
Where was Jesus? _____
Who did he call and how many? _____
Whom were they to be with? _____
What did He appoint them to be? _____
What were they to do?_____

The twelve Apostles were called out from among the other disciples to be with Jesus in a close everyday walk with Him. Learning from Him as they went from place to place sharing life together. In fact, their close proximity to Him was to teach them to be like their Rabbi – Jesus. As they spent time with Him, they would become like Him.

You may have started to notice that there has been a progression numerically narrowing down the scale of people coming 'nearer' to Jesus. A reducing, tightening and trimming down from the multitudes to the 72. Then down to the 12.

Read Mark 14:32-34:
Where were Jesus and His disciples and what did He ask them to do in **verse 32**?

_____

Who did Jesus take even closer with Him? _____   _____   _____

What happened to Jesus and what did He say to them?
_____

Even though the Apostles traveled with Him everywhere, when it came to our Lord's most distressing time He appealed to and beckoned for the closer companionship of Peter, James, and John. Jesus asked them to stick by His side and pray. Ultimately they were not able to be there for Him. Each time Jesus came back to check in with them they had fallen asleep. At Jesus' greatest time of need, only His Father was authentically there for Him in the end.

All of us have had times when we have felt abandoned and alone because no human could authentically be there with us in our darkest moments either. Only our Father.

I kept myself protected from other people's ability to hurt my heart if they rejected me. Especially the rejection in which they didn't care for something about me, even something I couldn't really change. Being vulnerable in my weaknesses has been incredibly difficult for me. I feared what others would think of me. This strong yet false power controlled many of the choices I made. I craved closer companions to walk with during my deep valleys. But, even though I have asked others into my inner sanctum, to stick by my side and pray, my expectations of them led me to think they abandoned me when they 'fell asleep.' People couldn't and can't be there for me all the time. They don't even have the capacity to do that. It has been a maturing process for me as I have earnestly clung to the Lord and eased up on my expectations of others. Most of the time people have truly meant well, and I have grown to see it wasn't rejection, they are overwhelmed with their own hurts, needs, and struggles.

As you think about choosing to go to the top with Jesus, to have the ultimate intimacy you yearn for with your Covenant Partner, have you thought whether there could be a cost? It is something to consider. The cost may be, that the closer you get to the top the fewer traveling companions you may have along the way. As you undergo life's trials and stress and most especially during your emotionally dark and draining times, first you won't have the energy to reach out to many for comfort. And second, you may not want to share right at that moment the depth of what you are experiencing. (This can also be true of the most splendid joyous moments in your life.)

One of the ways I know that I am up on 'top of the mountain' with the Lord is that during these moments I can sense that God is there with me during my crisis. The one thing I need more than anything else is His presence.

In Exodus 33:15 Moses knew the unsearchable value of God's presence.

Moses said, **"If your presence does not go with us, do not send us up from here. How will anyone know that you are pleased with me and with your people unless you go with us? What else will distinguish me and your people from all the other people on the face of the earth?"**

That is what awaits us at the top! **His Presence!!**

Putting this together:

Unlike going to the top in this world of our career or to the top of our game, the top here means something more spectacular.

God showed up one day, out of the blue, in a bush on fire with His presence. Moses drew close; God drew closer still. The Elders, Aaron and his two sons were granted a different type of access based on their positions as leaders and workers for God. In Moses's time, there was strict barriers and protocol set, and permission was needed to climb to the top of the mountain.

The barrier has been torn down, blood spilled, and access to approach has been approved because of Jesus. When we draw close, God draws closer still, even more intensely as He fills us with Himself – the protocol of the Kingdom to enter into the tangible presence of our wonderful King is worship. **We can have the level of either worker or worshiper**. It depends on us. Remember we have been invited to dine at the King's table.

> "Consumers eat at the King's table with only the occasional obligatory nod toward the King Himself. Consuming his blessings, they love His gifts – His power, His provision – but do they love Him? On the other hand, worshipers nibble at the same table, totally focused on the King."
> Tommy Tenney

Can I share a secret with you? This is what it means to go to the top!

We usually spend so much time seeking His stuff, working so hard for Him, that we don't have time and don't know what to do to be with Him. We are more concerned about the presents than the Presence. More concerned about getting the job done – sometimes designed and implemented by our own self-effort.

Worship is to express love. To be focused. Focused on the One, our One and only One. Remember from Week 2 our definition for determined was focus:

Determination = Covenant
Determination = Focus

Focus = Worship

Whatever you focus on is actually what you worship.

So if it is all the work that must be done for either you or God, then that is what you worship. If your focus is the King than He is Whom you worship.

I began learning this that day at the river. It sure has been a journey. I said yes to God and have been following His lead into the secret realm of His heart (the top of the mountain). God has captured my heart. I want to be a worshiper, pouring my adoring devotion onto Jesus for Who He is. To be a priest ministering to the heart of God, this has become my greatest passion!

But honestly, no matter how long we have been a Christian we are not immune from burnout - emotional, physical or spiritual.

1. It can be the reason why we are so disillusioned.
2. It can be why we are not feeling His love.
3. It can be why we are so exhausted from striving...

Despite my true intentions...

Third

The pressure was causing my right arm to feel like it was going to explode. The electronic machine had no idea the pain it was causing me as it just kept squeezing harder and harder. The report from the doctor was, your blood pressure is sky high. 210/109. Take this under your tongue, lay down for 20 minutes and we will take your blood pressure again. Still very high, she repeated the process. I could tell by the look on her face that something was wrong. She asked me if I had been under any unusual stress or anxiety. My life had felt like only stress and anxiety for a few years. So my answer was, "Well, a ton of complex, worrisome issues had attacked our family, and all of us were feeling the pinch." She had been my doctor for a few years, so she knew a few of the topics that had surfaced in health related areas.

She had me call my husband to take me home, and explained to him that I either had to go to the hospital right then or he would need to bring me back twice a week to be monitored. Of course, I chose the latter. She put me on some medication, with the diagnosis of fibromyalgia, high blood pressure, anxiety that was fight-or-flight and Mononucleosis at age 50 (really?). And it is interesting - God's timing. I got laid off from my job that next week, now I had time to 'recover.' In the next six weeks, I lost 20 pounds a lot for my small frame (one of the only perks). I felt numb, old, and distanced from people. The darkness that I was experiencing had been brewing for a long time. When it erupts, it just spews forth. I had been stuffing, stuffing and doing more stuffing of most of the things in my life. I didn't want anyone to see me as weak. I had spent so much time measuring my self-worth by how others viewed me. Now I was in crisis, and since I had put on the stoic, everything is alright persona. I didn't want to be with anyone. I didn't want anyone to see me this way and how could I explain to them what was going on when I was struggling to understand it myself.

At one of my subsequent doctor visits, she spent some time trying to tell me I was depressed. "Who me, no way. Christians don't get depressed we have to trust in God." She said she was leaving me in the room for a while to think about what I had just said and would return after she was finished with her next patient. A bit later she poked her head in to see if I had accepted the obvious yet. I had to reach into my soul to discover that I felt as though I was being forced down under water and held there against my will by despair, hopeless-ness, and sadness. Not at God, of course. He is kind and loving (that would come later). No, the real issue was me. I hated me. During the previous years, I had been wrestling with 'who I am.' Nothing I did felt like it was right or enough. I saw myself through the lens of everything I had ever done wrong. A chilling fear crept over me and seemed to invade my being as I embarked on what turned out to be a long, dark winter of the soul.

None of us seek out pain in our lives, but when we find ourselves in that awful bleak place, it becomes time to pay attention to what God wants to say to us in the darkness. Part of my problem was that I believed if I started to cry I would never stop, so I built a wall around my emotions. I found out that depression sits on us when we look back over all that has happened.

I took long walks, some at the park near my house, others up high in the hills nearby. As I would walk I had my headphones on, worship music playing and my eyes were usually just staring down at the ground. As I would pass people going the other way at the park, I would avoid eye contact because I felt so dark and hated myself so much that I didn't want anyone to see into my eyes.

The reasons for this kind of darkness vary from person to person. I had the agonizing heartaches that feel as if they bury you alive. Maybe you have had them as well. If I listed them to you they might seem ordinary or maybe to you they might seem as though they are not that big of a deal in comparison to yours. And I understand that. I will share it from the mere fact of the consecutive intensity of one right after the other. As they started pulverizing my sense of stability, it felt as if I couldn't breathe between each crisis. Job loss, big move to a different state after most of life in one place, untold health emergencies (brother major heart attack at age 38, father-in-law quadruple by-pass surgery, mother-in-law stage 3 colon cancer and I have already mentioned my mother and father). Major financial problems with home loss, bankruptcy and the daily stress of not enough to live on after years of countless blessing. Many rejections from family and friends, things that can't be shared because of other peoples' privacy, stress at work, and a deep longing for ministry that had yet to be fulfilled. These things and just life, in general, had started to creep up and take a toll on my last ditch effort to hold it together. Even a church that I was a member of, taught studies at and spoke at for a conference 'dismembered' me when they changed pastors because I was unable to attend as regularly as they deemed necessary to be a member. It is funny how the overload can only go so far before that one thing is the bursting point. That kicker for me was being told by the leader of a Bible study I had been attending for nine years, "If you come back, there will be women who don't want to come anymore." Sitting there right after receiving that news I couldn't breathe, I couldn't move. It was as if all the wind was knocked out of me and would never be coming back. I had no idea what I had done and to whom or why. I spent weeks curled up in the fetal position in bed with an agony in my gut that unless you have felt it, there can be no words to describe how that ache feels, the deep pain of rejection. Shockingly, I found out later that it was because a few women didn't like my love for God. They thought that I thought, He loved me so much. Each of us is loved by Him and isn't that the point?

Well, this left me in the place of feeling misunderstood. This is the cup of misunderstanding. This cup is different than other cups because it tastes very bitter and must be drunk alone. Each drop has the savor of injustice and leaves an overwhelming sinking feeling in your stomach - blindsided. It has a slow release feature, in that the full swig of it isn't felt immediately. Yes, it hurts from the first sip, but it is what happens over the next days and weeks that gets you! It haunts you with torment following you into almost every area of who you are. This cup is especially harsh if delivered from a brother or sister in Christ, or anyone close to you. The problem is that any attempt to sweeten the bitter taste by justification or defensiveness only backfires. The only choice is to drink it and choose to love. These women had misjudged my motives, and the wound was devastating. When you get excluded from a Bible study that seems to feel like the lowest of lows, "Not even good enough for that"... I began to question my very existence. Shame paralyzed me.

Shame is much more damaging than guilt. Guilt tells you that you have **done** something wrong, shame tells you that you **are** something wrong. Shame is even more of an emotion than anger. All my life I would have the fear that I was in trouble. I would get this dread in my stomach and nausea waves throughout my body every time someone would confront me. Terrified of what they might say or want, and deathly worried I had done some huge offense. Shame burdens us to measure our worth by our doing. As long as we listen to it, we will have a distorted view of ourselves and all that is around us. (But its voice can be unmasked, dropping our mask we won't have to pretend.)

During this dark winter, I was being stripped down naked literally and emotionally. I didn't shower for days, put no makeup on and wore old, worn-out, tattered clothes, in fact, I wore the very same thing most of the time. All of this being extremely unusual for me. I felt as though I was reducing down to the bare minimum, the minimum of who I was, so I could see who I really am.

My façade of the sometimes held together fake smile, beautifully manicured nails, hair, dress, and jewelry, was a disguise to hide behind. Perfectionism had become a barrier between the other women and me; the very women I so longed to love, encourage in life and walk with together in the Lord. How could they measure up to someone with all 'that glory'? God allowed all these circumstances so I would come to the end of pretending.

Fourth

It's funny how the things that bring you to the end of your rope can bring you to the end of yourself. During this prolific shedding process, some women were so tender, loving and believed in me. Each one of them has a special spot in my heart that is filled to overflowing with sincere gratitude. These 11 women would gather in my family room each Monday night. I had met most of them the year before, teaching an evening study. They accepted me for who I was in that very state of despair and physical exhaustion. There were evenings, however, that I was so strung out that I would have to take a Xanax just to show up in my own home.

The first half of the year we did a study on prayer. How ironic since I had a lump form in my throat preventing me from praying out loud for a very long time. But I learned that one of the most wonderful aspects of our relationship with Jesus is that we don't have to talk — He just understands. He sees it all and knows what is going on from every vantage point imaginable — no explanations needed. Such a fabulous thing when you are just too exhausted even to feel.

The second half of the year we did a study, that I would have to say, is by far the most impactful one I have ever done. The Lord and I wrote this study; it was the first version of the study you are currently working through. The reason I say it is the best study is that of the magnitude of the topic. As we were reviewing this week after week with each other, the Lord was reinforcing what I needed to hear again, God's Covenant of Love. His Love, the most powerful force on the planet.

After I finally acknowledged how excruciating the depth of the shame, dread and hatred toward myself had been, God had His plan to restore me – better, more gentle and tender in heart – more like Jesus. I spent time concentrating on getting my health back, by eating better, taking vitamins, and I joined a gym, and I went – a lot. What a great stress and anxiety reliever. I have had to own up to the fact that for now, I need to take depression medication, a stigma in the Christian world because there is a strong belief that we don't need to treat our brains medically. The real truth is that our brain is an organ of our body and sometimes needs medication, just like the kidney or any other organs that aren't functioning correctly. There is a difference between our brain and having 'the mind of Christ.' So if you suffer from depression don't let anyone tell you just to ignore it.

At first, I struggled with concentration, so reading was difficult. But as the Lord was healing me I found myself reading one book after the other – on God's Love. I also read books on the Law and freedom, liberty and our new life in Christ. I had been suffocating under the weight of too many Christian rules, principles, performance or whatever anyone wants to call it. What I needed was to be drenched in God's grace. It is amazing how we hold ourselves hostage bound by the covenant of Law, when Jesus died on the cross, rose from the grave, ascended to heaven to give us freedom in Him. If we are living the life that is truly life, it is Jesus plus nothing!

I started getting up the nerve to tell my big secret, a nervous breakdown, to someone outside of my immediate circle of family and friends. It was difficult at first to pull the veil off my pride in front of my own family. But I mustard up the courage to disclose what I thought may have the potential to ruin me – as a Bible study leader, wife of a wonderfully supportive husband who is on staff at a church. Could this have caused problems for him – who knows what the ramification could have been but I chose my first person and made the call. He was someone I had worked with, shared an office with and trusted in his heart towards me. It was the start. God kept giving me more and more bravery. This part of the healing process took many months.

Fifth

The love of God heals our soul! He will never love me more than right at this moment. He will never love you more than right at this very moment. He loves because He is love and because He is good. It is so important that we know we are loved. Own that love, embrace that love, and jump into the arms of that love. It is right in the Bible that this is an understood fact.

Please read John 13:21-25:

Jesus was with His disciples sharing the future event of His betrayal by Judas Iscariot.

Why was Jesus troubled in spirit in **verse 21**?_____

What was the disciples' reaction? _____

Isn't that incredible? None of them had any idea there could have been someone in their close-knit group that could betray their Lord. The love of the Lord is so great that He holds out hope, all of the time, to the point that no one else would know by His reaction that there was a problem with anyone else's heart.

Write out verse 23 below:

_____

_____

What did Simon Peter motion and ask this disciple to do in **verse 24**?

_____

How did he ask Jesus, what was his position in **verse 25**?

_____

Who wrote **this** book of the Bible, the book of John? _____
What do you think about the fact that John called himself the disciple whom Jesus loved?

_____

What does that say about his relationship with Jesus?

_____

Could you call yourself that? _____
Why or why not?

_____

There are a few other places in the gospel of John where he referred to himself in this way, John 19:26 and John 20:2. In the later verse John puts it this way, **"So she came running to Simon Peter and the other disciple, the one Jesus loved…"**. In other words, he spoke of himself as being esteemed and delighted in by God. To be the apple of God's eye, to be loved tenderly.

No other gospel says that, just his. He called **himself** that. He spoke that over his own life. He knew he was accepted. "I am accepted and that is what I am – beloved". He realized his true identity in Christ.

John didn't seem to grapple with his identity.

That has been a strain for me. "I am your beloved!" —— How easily do those words roll off your tongue?

We think of Jesus as the Beloved:
At Jesus' baptism, He went down into the water, and when He came up the heavens opened and John saw the Spirit of God descending like a dove and alighting on Him.

Please read this next scripture (provided):
"And behold, a voice from heaven said, 'This is my Son, my beloved, in whom I delight!"' Matthew 3:17

At the Jordan River, God chose these words you just read to describe Jesus. And then, right away Jesus was led into the wilderness to be tempted and tested by Satan. The first time the enemy showed up notice what he said to Jesus.

Please read this next scripture (provided):
"And the tempter came and said to him, If you are God's Son, command these stones to be made bread."

What words did Satan leave out in this verse that were in the Mathew 3:17 verse (on the previous page)?

_____

The enemy has spent much of my life in the Lord doing this to me. Making me think that '**My beloved**' is taken out. The moment I remember my identity in Christ as His beloved – Satan won't be able to succeed. In the past, the enemy has used other people to confront me on this, jealous or something. But, it isn't something to be jealous of in anyone else, it isn't something to be prideful of on our part either. No, it is just the reality!!

Here is the real truth…

> **My identity is the Lord's love for me and I am His beloved**.

It applies to you as well!! Isn't that fabulous!

The following two passages in the New Testament describe us as the beloved:

"To you then all God's beloved ones in Rome, called to be saints and designated for a consecrated life." Romans 1:7

"So that we might be to the praise and the commendation of His glorious grace, favor and mercy, which He so freely bestowed on us in the Beloved." Ephesians 1:6

The Lord showed me this too:
When you know that you are God's beloved, you will be able to take down all the giants in your life! Wow! All the lies will be removed because the truth is they can't be together with who I am in Him. I mentioned that wanting to be popular has been my lure. It kept me from the truth because I compared myself to others. I stacked myself up to what the Lord was doing in someone else's life and it sometimes just didn't seem fair. It didn't always feel like love, shattered by this lie my insecurity mounted when I was not thought of by others as I would have cherished. But my identity isn't in them...

"My identity is God's love for me!"

Say that out loud to yourself as often as you need to believe it.

Knowing this has revolutionized my thinking, my constant languishing was stilled the moment this genuinely sank into my heart. The end of the fear of being found out. What I mean is….. We all struggle with something that we think defines us and if anyone ever found out about it, we feel we would no longer be accepted. That's how I felt before God touched my heart with the knowledge of my true identity.

We finish this week with this…

That day at the river years ago I was reading Ezekiel 16. That section of Scripture has been a hallmark in my walk with Him. That same passage says this in verse 8 (an allegory for Jerusalem, but it applies to us as well).

"Later I passed by, and when I looked at you and saw that you were old enough for love, I spread the corner of my garment over you and covered your nakedness. I gave you my solemn oath and entered into a covenant with you, declares the Sovereign Lord, and you became mine."

Outrageous!! It seriously takes by breath away every time I read this or think about it. And God gave His solemn oath.

What did you enter into? _____

What did you become? _____

In covenant, you became His. "I am Yours Jesus!" - "I am Yours Jesus!"

The song 'Remind Me Who I Am' by Jason Gray was one of the hit songs on the radio during this dark winter of my soul. It was also our theme worship song for the group of women who met at my house weekly. We loved to praise the Lord together singing this song with great enthusiasm standing gathered in a circle around my coffee table in my family room. Let this song minister to you, listen to or read the words.

Go online and listen while you read!
Jason Gray— "Remind me who I am"

When I lose my way,
And I forget my name
Remind me who I am
In the mirror all I see
Is who I don't wanna be
Remind me who I am

In the loneliest places
When I can't remember what grace is

Tell me, once again
Who I am to You, who I am to You
Tell me, lest I forget
Who I am to You, that I belong to You
To You

When my heart is like a stone,
And I'm running far from home
Remind me who I am
When I can't receive Your love
Afraid I'll never be enough
Remind me who I am

If I'm Your **beloved** can You help me believe it

Tell me, once again
Who I am to you, who I am to You
Tell me, lest I forget
Who I am to you, that I belong to You

I'm the one You love, I'm the one You love
That will be enough, I'm the one You love

Tell me, once again
Who I am to you, who I am to You
Tell me, lest I forget
Who I am to you, that I belong to You

It is ok to be who you are. And It is ok to be ok with who you really are. The Lord loves you for you! He wants you to know who you already are in Him so you can have a deeper, fuller and higher up on the mountain top relationship with Him. Now in the New Covenant because of Jesus and in His grace, He is always waiting for you to come up higher, and to draw nearer.

Worship is the force thrusting you to **'The Top.'**

Next week

We conclude our study together……

Week 7

Fully Persuaded

Last week

We saw what the cost might be to have this incredible intimacy with the Lord. The closer we get to the top of the mountain the fewer close traveling companions we may have along the way, and this is not necessarily a bad thing because what we receive at the top is the Lord's presence. Worship is the force thrusting us to 'The Top.' The Lord meets us in an incredible way as we learn that we are His beloved.

There may be some circumstances that seem to draw us closer to the Lord and even catapult us straight into His arms. I shared my story about what led to my new awareness of my identity in the Lord. After years of tumultuous circumstances and my pretending that everything was fine, I reached rock bottom and hit the wall of despair. The Lord was bringing me to the end of myself, to the end of pretense, to the end of the fear of being found out. He was showing me that it was ok to be real, ok to share my weaknesses with others and that I didn't have to meet everyone's expectations. That my identity is God's love for me.

It is also true that your identity is God's love for you! I hope that you are discovering more intensely that you are His and His beloved. I pray you will learn that your identity is God's love for you in a much less painful way than I had to learn it.

This week

We find ourselves in our final week together. My heart is just overflowing with love for all of you, even though I may not have met you or ever will. Thank you from the bottom of my heart for permitting me to share my story so openly with you – as you have continued to read and complete this study to the finale. God's love story is beautiful both in His covenant with Abraham and now with us. We conclude with Romans 8. Paul explains to us what he discovered and what gave him the unequivocal assurance of the depth of God's love. The Lord Jesus is the ultimate Lover of our soul. Intimately acquainted with every aspect of our lives, our heart and each breath we take. His love is the most wonderfully compelling thing I have ever known and felt. God has captivated me. A.W. Tozer put it so eloquently:

> "To be filled with moral excitement; to be captivated and charmed and entranced with who God is, and struck with astonished wonder at the unconceivable elevation and magnitude and splendor of Almighty God. To love God with all the power within me, to love God with fear and wonder and yearning and awe. At times this will lead to breathless silence." A.W. Tozer

Getting Ready:

Please allow yourself to be an open vessel. To hear the still small voice of the Lord, to hear the messages He is avidly and tenaciously pouring out constantly upon our hearts, we must be observant. He comes and enlightens upon the core of our being and the essence of our thought life. With eager anticipation, we can receive from Him the details we might otherwise miss if we are just unwittingly going about our life. This last week of study has buried treasure that, to be honest, has taken me the majority of my life to gain the needed multifaceted eyes to see into these nuggets of radiant gold. I pray we will all see Him with new eyes, and enjoy Him with a new affection.

Let's define covenant:

Please go back to the first week and on the lines below write out the exact definition we started out with for our study.

_____

_____

_____

First

Think about what you have been viewing – God's True Love. His perfect plan to **redeem** you. To bring you back, to call you His own. How glorious He is, Jesus the Redeemer.

The word 'covenant' in the Old Testament is the Hebrew word 'berith' and is used some 286 times in various contexts. However, the meaning and weight of this word come down to the idea of 'bond' relating to its root 'bara' that means 'to bind.'

"I pray that out of his glorious riches he may strengthen you with power through faith. And I pray that you, being rooted and established in love, may have power, together with all the saints, to grasp how wide and long and high and deep is the love of Christ, and to know this love that surpasses knowledge – that you may be filled to the measure of all the fullness of God." Ephesians 3:16-19

These four verses sum up the importance of covenant and why we have spent weeks engrossed in this particular kind of love. Every day that you awaken with a sense of dissatisfaction in your life that is deeply permeating your soul, it could very well be that you have been looking around trying to find the missing piece of the puzzle. This missing piece is found when you link covenant love and rooted together.

As you observe the scripture above I hope that it will help you to see how important being rooted in love, the right love is. The puzzle piece is God's covenant love. His brilliant love is like no other. The moment you compare His love to any other love in your life, the other will pale in comparison because nothing comes remotely close. I don't know about you, but I do not want to be **rooted** in a love that can't love me the way I have to be loved. I say 'have to be loved' because we have to know that Someone **TOTALLY** loves us.

We spend so much energy looking, searching, chasing and clawing our way through life putting our hopes and dreams into love that isn't True Love. But as you keep discovering (which I pray with all of my heart you are) this kind of love that captivates, this kind of love that draws you in, you will begin to be fully immersed and rooted in the confidence of the One who established this bond. Have you been chasing after love, have you been chasing after dreams? If you are in this covenant with the Lord, this two-sided relationship then you already have your dream and the greatest treasure, love beyond reason.

The morning after I was up late reading a book, I thought my mind was playing tricks on me. What I thought I first observed in black and white on the page of that book turned out to not be there the next morning. I had gone back to journal what God had revealed to me the night before. And as I turned to that page it said something completely different than what I thought it said.

Like many of you, I have chased after my dreams. They seem at times to run faster in front of me with each passing year of my life. The moment I think I am reaching out to catch one of these dreams they look as if they disappear out of sight.

Think for a moment of the biggest dream you have in or for your life. What have you always dreamed about doing or being? It may be hard to write it down, but its ok **put it to print below:**

_____

_____

Maybe it is your dream man or woman, or a dream job, a house, an adventure, or maybe even the dream of a vibrant ministry for the Lord. Or maybe it is just freedom from your sense of inadequacy.

I have had one dream in particular (I won't share what it is, so it won't clutter up your mind and keep you from thinking about your dream). Has your dream ever eaten away at you? It has in me. It has driven me crazy.

The Lord is asking us, both of us – has this dream become an idol? We must put it on the altar, like Isaac.

Late that night I heard the Lord tell me in my heart – you already have your dream.

"What? No way Lord." Again I heard Him clearly reveal to me that I already have my dream.

As I sat up higher in my bed, I could feel the touch of the Lord – I am your Dream! Dream with a capital 'D.' You have the fullness of My love. Stop striving for some other dream, what could ever be more fulfilling than being filled to the full measure of God. "Yes Lord. I rest in Your love. I rest in any purpose or dream You have for me because You are my Dream!"

I guess I saw words on that page differently than they were so that the Lord could convey to me a truth that would set me free. The Lord got my attention. He let me vividly comprehend what my true dream is, Him. I am indeed rooted in knowing I have what I have always wanted, You Lord Jesus, You! I am rooted and anchored in Your love.

My identity is God's love for me!

Sometimes it takes a while for us to fully comprehend and be fully persuaded of the depth of a concept that seems too good to be true.

On the other hand, we have read of Abraham, who had witnessed the fulfillment of God's promises over and over again. Abraham had built up his faith to the place that when God came to him with the 'big one' (Isaac was his dream), he was capable (in God's grace) to be persuaded that God could and would do what He promised.

Please read Romans 4:18-21:

When there seemed to be no hope what was it that Abraham demonstrated in **verse 18**? _____

What does **verse 19** say about his faith? He didn't do what? _____

Again it reiterates this point in **verse 20** what does that verse say he didn't do? _____

He was strengthened in his faith and gave glory to God.

Write out verse 21 below:

_____

_____

Abraham was fully persuaded. He knew God had fulfilled His promises in the past. These verses in Romans speak of how Abraham decided to view things from God's perspective rather than from the way we usually see things in the natural. We are pessimistic as humans, and our tendency is to see the negative and hang onto it. But no matter what the circumstances may look like to us we can cling to hope.

I had to search inside my soul to know if I was believing God or in some way pretending with false hope. God asked me the question, "Are you fully persuaded like Abraham?"

Are you?

I had to admit that sometimes I do allow how things seem to look all around me to dictate whether I believe God and what He says. Abraham did not. He believed. It is interesting that Abraham did not pretend as if the circumstances in his life did not exist. The Apostle Paul says Abraham 'faced the fact' that neither he nor

Sarah was likely to bear a child given their ages. Facing that reality did not weaken his faith. It strengthened it. Abraham was fully persuaded; 'that God had the power to do what He had promised.'

Not a little bit persuaded or even mostly persuaded, but **fully** persuaded!

Just as Abraham was fully persuaded that God's almighty power could accomplish anything, we can be too. However, if you are like me, you may at times believe God is doing great miracles in other people's lives, but you are not witnessing much of this for yourself in your life yet. The Lord can do the impossible for anyone, including you and me. Sometimes, just as Abraham had to do, we must wait for God's timing. We will go through a specific process to step into the promise. We learn not to waver, and our belief is strengthened during that process.

Second

I sometimes have wavered in the process as I shared with you last week. None of us are perfect. Although Abraham was fully persuaded, he was human too.

After the Lord was bringing me up out of that huge pit of despair and darkness, I could sense a mounting freedom brewing, but I knew that there was nonetheless a part of me that was still resistant to the totality of this particular kind of perfect love.

Just when I thought the dust might be settling, it happened...

The spirals of more confusing life altering and gut-wrenching events and circumstances just kept coming down the pike, one after the other.

But how could these be from God I thought.....

How could this come from the God I thought I knew loved me? If this was the way God loved me, what kind of love is this anyway? The more I seemed to love Him the more I kept feeling my life was caving in. "Why God?"

A few months went by, and I was reeling in agony as to why it sure didn't feel as though God loved me. Then it struck!!

I had asked my youngest daughter to have her room straightened up by the time I got home. When I arrived she and her dog were fast asleep on her bed, room untouched. I think I blew a gasket or something. I just exploded. She woke up in a startle, pretty much freaking out as to why I was on such a tirade. I turned around and slammed her bedroom door as hard as I could into the back wall. It made a huge hole that lined up perfectly with the doorknob. Then I progressed to the garage where I just lost it! I screamed so loud the whole neighborhood could have heard it. Then I bolted my way back inside slamming that door backward so hard it made a gaping hole in that wall too.

I felt out of my mind, reeling in hurt.

I ran into my bedroom shut the door and fell to the floor weeping. All the tears I had pent up behind my wall of emotion were let loose. I sobbed… there aren't words to describe what I was feeling or what emotions were rising in me. I could almost see my life flash before my eyes as I revisited all the overwhelming things I thought were a lack of love from God in my life.

The next thing I knew I was denouncing God and everything He had and had ever offered. I honestly wanted nothing ever to do with Him again. I took my beloved Bible of 20 plus years and threw it as rigorously as I could across the room at the wall. It hit hard and fell to a crumpled mess on the floor. I didn't care. I was done.

Therefore there is now no condemnation for those who are in Christ Jesus…

Please read Romans 8:1-4:
This first verse is one that many of us know in part and maybe even by heart.

Write out verse 1 below:

_____

_____

What does the word condemnation mean to you?

_____

Why are you and I free from condemnation according to **verse 2**?

_____

We already learned that the Law in itself is powerless. How did God send His Son in **verse 3**?

_____

What did God do by sending His Son in **verses 3 & 4**?

_____

Explain what has been met in order for you and me, to no longer live under condemnation in **verse 4**?

_____

_____

" The mind of sinful man is death, but the mind controlled by the Spirit is life and peace: the sinful mind is hostile to God. It does not submit to God's law, nor can it do so." Romans 8:6-7

Even though there is now no condemnation and we have a new heart in Christ, our minds can still betray us. We can live questioning our position in freedom. And live questioning God's goodness because of our mind-set.

The big question is, "Do I believe God to be good or bad?"

Do I subconsciously believe in my mind that God could be even a bit cruel doing even the smallest evil or tiniest unscrupulous thing?

Do you?

From my journal:

"Lord, I can ascertain by my doubts and complaints, hurt feelings, overwhelmed demonstrations and all my expectations that I have been attributing to You a base character that I would not want to have attributed to me. As I think about it Lord, nothing grieves me more than to have my family and friends misjudge and misunderstand me or my motives. I sure don't want to be accused of what I seem to have attributed to You. You have changed my heart to be more and more like Yours. I don't intentionally set out to do harm. So, could I ever for one instant believe that You would either."

*"But, am I confident that You are **completely** and **wholly** good?"*

"Lord, I have definitely discerned that other sources have ulterior motives for my life. The enemy, life, the Fall, and people's choices all around me affect my life. These are not designed to hurt me or make my life miserable. But somehow You take all of the bad trials, problems, and tribulations and make a new me."

Have you heard of the word providence?

The word providence has been such a hard word for me to remember over the years. It seems to be right on the tip of my tongue, and my brain is straining to remember it. I want to say prosperity because we hear so much on this. But providence is deeper. God is the provider to His creation, and thus His providence is significant for the life of man. "The Lord will provide" is seen throughout scripture. It is interesting that this must of necessity be confirmed in faith. We have to come to the belief that God is the sustainer of all He has entrusted to Himself. To sit back and marvel at the continuous physical existence of the sustained incomprehensible mighty power of God.

Providence, however, is not looking at the world and all that is around us with rose colored glasses.

We know that there are many problems, evil, and much suffering and pain. Instead, it is profound realism. Accepting a situation and being prepared to handle it authentically, practically and pragmatically. We have a choice; we can attempt to view a situation through the ever wavering lens of fate and fortune. And if we put that into our current trending way of saying it, then that would be called 'karma.' That is the idea that whatever happens is by chance and what goes around comes around and decides our future 'existences.' This speculative philosophy is far from the doctrine and theology of providence. The divine providence of God is revealed and attested to in and throughout all of Scripture. If we believe God, it should enable those that trust in His preservation to be capable of living a life free from anxiety, because a good Father will espouse to care for His children all of the time, faithfully.

Is the passive acceptance of everything being the will of God correct?

Why then is there this thinking and teaching, that is truthfully so prevalent it makes your head spin, that says, "Nothing can happen unless God wills it to happen?" We've been taught through the misinterpreting of Scripture that, "God ordained it and this thing is given to work toward our higher good." In other words, behind every event, God has an ulterior motive and a particular purpose and thus it would not have happened unless God willed it. The reason why everything takes place is God, and evil somehow fits into God's overall plan for good, so He authors it? Car wrecks, cancer, divorce are hard to comprehend, and we give pat answers like, "There's purpose in everything. He is sovereign remember."

Is this true?

Please read Romans 8:28-29 (provided):
You may think you know what these verses say, but I ask you to read them slowly and thoughtfully.

"And we know that in all things God works for the good of those who love him, who have been called according to his purpose. For those God foreknew he also predestined to be conformed to the likeness of his Son, that he might be the firstborn among many brothers."

God works in all things but are all things from God? Then this would have to include evil. Then, God would be behind all evil. By reason we would have to attribute God to cause fear and for Him to have a malicious side. He would be set about to discipline us and have us learn our lesson. How could we ever be able to trust or know what He is going to do next? Then this could lead to doubting God's true nature.

Please read Romans 8:15-17:
What did you NOT receive according to **verse 15**?

_____

This is fascinating! You did not receive a Spirit that makes you a slave **again** to fear. The Law made us slaves, and fear keeps us hostage. That is the way it was in the Old Covenant at Mt Sinai, do good get good, do bad get bad. Performance based. God never wanted the terrified grind and duty of slaves. And now that Jesus Christ has set us free from the Law and condemnation we shouldn't want to go back to 'Egypt.'

What have you received now in **verse 15**?

_____

What do we cry? _____

We have a new Father – an Abba Father – a Daddy and we are His children, His heirs.

Jesus showed us God the Father. **"Jesus answered: "Don't you know me, Philip, even after I have been among you such a long time? Anyone who has seen me has seen the Father. How can you say, 'Show us the Father'? Don't you believe that I am in the Father, and the Father is in me? Rather, it is the Father, living in me, who is doing his work."** John 14:9-10.

Jesus was the exact representation of the Father (as seen in Hebrews 1:3). When Jesus walked on earth, He challenged disaster, disease, and troubles as though He was confronting a battleground. He came to reveal the heart of the Father. To rescue the victimized to show mercy and compassion on the brokenhearted and the sick. He came as though something was terribly wrong, a work of an enemy! He didn't view everything that took place as the divine will of God. Instead, He brought healing and deliverance and relief.

Who are you an heir with in **Romans 8:17**? _____

What is the contingency, what do you have to share in in **verse 17**?

_____

What is the result of sharing in this? _____
So to share in the glory with the Lord, we first have to share in His sufferings?

From my journal:

"That is what all this has been about Lord? It has felt instead as if I was suffering because you didn't love me. You always know what is best and what is best for me – I truly have no clue. (Although I act like I know what is best)."

Look back at page 112 for Romans 8:28-29 for a moment:

We often leave out **Romans 8:29, please read it:**

Who are we being conformed into the likeness of? _____

To be conformed to the likeness of His Son, we have some changes that need to be made in our everyday life in the flesh. Remember your white robe of righteousness. You are still wearing this, so picture yourself again, pure, spotless and blameless; that is still how God sees you in Jesus. But, we sometimes sin, right? And some of our sins can negatively affect us, and we can also recognize our need to have some of the baggage from our past stripped away.

All of this conforming could be very painful at times. Because just as with clay, to mold something into a different shape it must sometimes be smashed and pounded and reshaped.

But, the finished work is a masterpiece of exquisite quality workmanship from the always loving hands of the greatest Potter.

Third

As we are being conformed to look like Jesus, we must discern who is wanting this in us and who is not. Those other sources we mentioned earlier can seem overpowering at times.

But we must remember this...

Please read Romans 8:31 (provided):

"What, then, shall we say in response to this? If God is for us, who can be against us?"

Who is for us? _____
Who can be against us? _____

Please jump forward a bit and read Romans 8:35:

This verse asks a question that is the key point of our study. Write out that question below:

_____

List the things in **verse 35** that follow that specific question.

_____

_____

The opposite of pure love is selfishness, greed, strife, jealousy, rage, hatred and chaos. People were given the freedom to have free-will and to choose and make decisions, leaving the door wide open for evil.

Why free-will then?

Because truthfully it is the only thing that makes any love or goodness worth having! Love must be chosen!

That brings with it the possibility of being rejected and for evil to be prevalent. Humanity has free-will. And what I understand now is that if we insist on our own way, then God in His permissive providence will let us have our way. This may cause waves of rippling torture to come as a natural consequence. Not only to us in ourselves but to all those that that decision effects. There is a difference between God's divine providence and His permissive providence. Both are going on in the world all around us at all times. He won't micromanage, and He does not put controls over and against anyone's free-will. And after the Fall the earth itself has been under this same bondage.

There will come a day when everything will be redeemed. Until then...

God is good period. He has His perfect providence over all He stands for!

(And He stands for love, truth, justice, equity, peace, joy, harmony, mercy and those things that are of His character of True Beauty.)

When we understand True Love, we will meet True Beauty.

The Bible says God is love!

"God is love. Whoever lives in love lives in God, and God in him." 1 John 4:16

"There is no fear in love. But perfect love drives out fear, because fear has to do with punishment." 1 John 4:18

God gave me a visual that I hope will help you as it did me.

A few days after my tirade, and after I 'took God back,' I was sitting on the floor in my bedroom with my back up against my bed. I had my iPod on as I was worshiping the Lord. This song from Christy Nockels just penetrated my being to the core. (If you haven't figured it out yet, I love music.)

Listen while you read!

HEALING IS IN YOUR HANDS by Christy Nockels

No mountain, no valley No gain or loss we know
Could keep us from Your love

No sickness, no secret No chain is strong enough
To keep us from Your love To keep us from Your love

How high? How wide? No matter where I am
Healing is in Your hands

How deep? How strong? Now by Your grace I stand
Healing is in Your hands

Our present, our future Our past is in Your hands
We're covered by Your blood
We're covered by Your blood

How high? How wide? No matter where I am
Healing is in Your hands

How deep? How strong? Now by Your grace I stand
Healing is in Your hands
In all things we know that we are more than conquerors
You keep us by Your love

In all things we know that we are more than conquerors
You keep us by Your love
You keep us by Your love

How high? How wide? Oh, Lord No matter where I am
Healing is in Your hands
How deep? How deep is Your love?
How strong? How strong is Your love?
Now by Your grace I stand
Healing is in Your hands

The words in this song come right out of Romans 8.

God had to sink the words to this song and these verses into my heart for life. My life depended on it. And then a few days later while working out at the gym on the treadmill, I was jogging listening to this song again. I felt a penetrating compulsion to keep pushing replay over and over for 30 minutes. I listened to this song with an unexplainable zeal growing. As it kept growing, I kept jogging faster and faster. Now I was running. I kept pushing replay on the accelerator button on the machine. Now I was full out running, fast, faster than I thought I could keep up with that belt that had no mercy. I sensed I was running to be set free to live in the reality of the words. Words that impacted me because I finally understood what it means to be fully persuaded.

*After being prayed for by Eric Scroggins (Week 5), he said, "You will know when you know." "When you are fully persuaded of God's **love** you will live free!"*

Please read Romans 8:37-39:

What 'these things' is **verse 37** referring to?

_____

What are we more than? _____
Through Whom? _____
What did He do? _____

How did God show His love? Let this truly sink in…He showed us the totality of His love through Jesus' death on the cross.

His death was the fulfillment of the Covenant He 'cut' with Himself.

The fulfillment of the Father and King Jesus passing through between the pieces changing history forever!!

Putting this together:

Read Romans 8:38:

What are the first four words of this verse?

_____

The Apostle Paul wrote this, and it says that he was more than a conqueror inwardly. He could go through these trials and emerge victorious because he was persuaded of something. Nothing could convince Him that God did not love him.

1) What was he convinced of, fill in the blanks below from Romans 8:38-39:

"Neither _____ nor life,
Neither angels nor _____.
Neither the present nor the _____, nor any powers
Neither _____ nor depth, nor anything _____ in all creation, will be able to
_____ us from the _____ of God that is in Christ Jesus our Lord."

Pretty powerful, isn't it? In the King James Version the words "For I am convinced" are these words, "For I am fully persuaded."

116

2) And, our study's key Ephesians passage:

"To grasp how wide and long and high and deep is the love of Christ, and to know this love that surpasses knowledge..." Ephesians 18-19

3) And now, putting this together with the words in the song:

> No mountain, no valley No gain or loss we know
> Could keep us from Your love
>
> No sickness, no secret No chain is strong enough
> To keep us from Your love To keep us from Your love
> Our present, our future Our past is in Your hands

I hope you are starting to see what I saw. Nothing can separate us from God's love. **Nothing!!**

Whatever life may hold, nothing compares to God's love. Somehow this made sense to me and I was confident. Fully persuaded. Persuaded of this truth - **God keeps me by His love**.

You see, I had been through major heartbreak to the point of utter brokenness, but what I discovered through the intensity of chaos, turmoil, striving, longing, fear, doubt, anxiety, insecurity, and the lowest of lows was the depth of the unrelenting love of God. The Father's delight in me at my most broken. No matter where I roam, even to the point of denouncing Him and His love, He is always good, and He is still loving me. No matter what!

Impossible? Amazing? Beautiful? Unquestionable! That is what I found.

Because of God's love, He chose to come to us as one of us. This is incredible love! We must realize that His approach toward us in covenant, as a man, was not out of desperation; it was not a plan B or just a last-ditch effort to save humanity. No, Jesus and the Father had this purposeful plan all along. This grand plan was done according to the love through what God established as 'covenant.' Something intended from the beginning. It gives me goose bumps to think of the heart behind this kind of pure perfect and beautiful love.

God is saying this to you…Listen to our definition of covenant from God's perspective...

"The most serious, sacred, and secure of all bonds, is the blood covenant. Its value is the closest, and the most enduring of promises. Without question, it can never be broken or altered because **I AM** permanently pledging **My** life, unconditional love, and protection to **you** forever."

"What is My root meaning behind the blood covenant?"

"We have entered into such a devoted and intimate relationship with each another that **everything I AM** and possess is offered without hesitating at any moment because of True Love."

Think of it this way:

We are so quick to put so much emphasis on either one or the other in a relationship. But this is a special union, a bond. Because of our human nature, our eyes naturally focus on ourselves, and as a result, we often struggle to focus on the Lord. That day at the river changed this in me, and immediately I so desired to learn to pour out my love to the Lord, God calls this worship.

To understand this two-sided relationship and the magnitude of God's love, the key is to see Jesus as a Person. When we accept that Jesus is a Person it makes our experience with Him tangible. Having a two-sided relationship with Him allows us to be real. No hiding, no pretending, no coercion. Just genuine friendship, fully realizing that this is a lasting unending forever bond and a union.

It is exciting to me to have the privilege of sharing all of who I am with God.

Do you remember what God called Abraham after He cut the covenant?

One of the parts of covenant partners was that they became friends.

Abraham was known as 'a friend of God.'

"And the scripture was fulfilled that says, "Abraham believed God, and it was credited to him as righteousness, and he was called God's friend." James 2:23

What wonderful news! We are in a friendship with Jesus. So instead of trying to figure out all of the rules, the lingo of Christianese, the opinions of one denomination over another, all of the correct theology, or simply trying to figure out whether we should go here and do this or that, whether to pray with our hands folded sitting or standing, or worrying about what we wear or what we should give, we can rest in the love of Jesus and our friendship with Him.

God has come all the way up to the edge of His side of the covenant by coming here and establishing covenant friendship. He loves you completely. There is nothing more secure than that God loves you. We sometimes have difficulty living it, knowing we are loved. And loved this much! You ARE!

Fourth

I would like for you to sit back for a moment and just take in this beautiful heart of love. Jesus is extraordinary! He is without comparison.

I want you to know that everything in me is just glued to this. For you to trust that you are **TOTALLY** loved, you must know the One who **TOTALLY** loves you. We have seen in Week 1 the steps of covenant and the human side of the covenant union of Jonathan and David. We have seen in Week 2 the cutting of covenant between Jesus and the Father and what part Abraham had in that covenant. His part remember was to believe. We have also seen the test that God put forth before Abraham. To lay down his long hoped-for and cherished son of the promise. Abraham went through with this until God intervened with a ram in the thicket as the sacrifice because it was not the right time. Much later it would be God's One and only beloved Son, Jesus. The Father and Jesus are **one**.

Look Who this love is...

~~~~~~It amazes me that He healed 10 lepers yet only one came back to love on Him in gratitude. He also healed a paralytic, a cripple woman, the demon-possessed, the blind and mute and the woman bleeding for 12 years. ~~~~~ He fed 5000 men at one sitting and 2000 at another. He walked on water, calmed storms, turned water into the finest wine at a wedding banquet. ~~~~~ He comforted little children and reached out to people with His gentle and humble heart. ~~~~~ He told many parables to give us an even greater insight into who He is and what His Kingdom resembles. Some of the other parables guide us in our daily life choices while others tell us how we need to behave in order to give Him delight and glory. ~~~~~ It is astounding that His resurrection power was seen here on earth as He raised at least three people from the dead, Lazarus, a widow's son, and Jairus' daughter. ~~~~~ He put the Sadducees and Pharisees in their place – opposing the proud and legalistic. He was the stumbling block to many. ~~~~~ He went away early in the morning to lonely places often to pray and spend time with His Father even after the whole town was gathered at His door late the night before. ~~~~~ He welcomed extravagant worship as perfume was poured on His feet and His head and worshiper's hair was used to wipe up the perfume. He could see the heart of people and could read their minds. He forgave. Yes, He is the only one who can forgive sin. ~~~~~ He overcame Satan in the desert! ~~~~~ He ate with tax collectors, tended to the poor, talked with Samaritans, healed on the Sabbath and spoke love over the sinner caught in adultery. He exhibited righteous anger as He turned over the tables of the money-changers at the Temple. ~~~~~ In keeping with covenant He had His last meal with His disciples the night before His crucifixion. Jesus predicted His own death. ~~~~~ He promised the Comforter would come – the Holy Spirit to guide us into all truth. He claimed to be the resurrection and the life, the I AM, the way the truth and the life. He said that if we had seen Him we had seen the Father in heaven, yet He washed His disciples' feet. ~~~~~ He wrestled with His flesh in the garden of Gethsemane and asked His Father to take the cup from Him but wanted the Father's will more than His own safety. ~~~~~ He was mocked and rejected and betrayed. He was whipped and flogged and beaten. He walked through the town almost naked and forsaken carrying His own instrument of death. He wore a crown of thorns instead of the crown of majesty. ~~~~~ He was nailed to a cross between two common thieves one who couldn't help but notice how amazing He was and the other who just didn't care. ~~~~~ The earth went dark from noon till 3:00. He was separated from the Father because of our sins. ~~~~~ He died the death of pure anguish and torture. People laughed and joked, and others cried and mourned. He was buried in a borrowed tomb. ~~~~~ He rose from the grave! Did you hear that? He rose from the grave once and for all conquering death. ~~~~~ He showed Himself to Mary Magdalene, His disciples and hundreds of others. ~~~~~ He

again demonstrated covenant as He ate a meal with His beloved disciples after His resurrection. ~~~~~~ He breathed on them and said, "Receive the Holy Spirit." ~~~~~~ He restored the regretful – Peter. ~~~~~~ He ascended into Heaven promising to come again to judge the earth. He is our High Priest, and He now intercedes for us.

Takes your breath away, doesn't He? I know you have been breathless as you have tried to take in Jesus (and not because of this somewhat lengthy description). But, wait!

I just can't get enough of Him, so please indulge me as I make a point of His powerful ministry and love forever wondrous for you – look at what John wrote as his very last sentence in his gospel.

Look up John 21:25:
Jesus did more... How many books would it take to contain what could be written about Jesus?

_____

It is hard for me to move. It is even harder for me to move on as I would just enjoy camping out in this section for a while longer marveling at our great King!!

Think about this...............True Love was born in a stable.

You and I are in covenant with this great King! The King of Glory!

Question for you. Which half of your covenant with God is stronger – your focus on you or your focus on Jesus?

_____

I shared with you that at the beginning of my relationship with the Lord, my focus was mostly on me. But my day at the river God showed me that a relationship is two-sided, what about Him? So I went from one extreme to the other. I put my emphasis on focusing on the majesty and greatness and love of the Lord, on His heart. On lifting Him up. And there is certainly nothing wrong with that. That should be our focus.

But, I learned something beautiful. I had been striving to live a life in which it was none of me and all of God. Does that sound like covenant?

No, a covenant is two-sided, a union, a bond. I now realize it is all about '**US**.'

The incredible immeasurable God of love wants me, and now I know that no matter what happens in my life I want Him too. Fully immersed in His love, that He keeps me by His love. A partnership involves both parties. In fact, I realized that I am not to dismiss 'me.'

In other words, if I hate myself...(or the opposite can be true as well, loving myself too much is also a problem of self).

If I hate myself how can I be one with my covenant partner? Partners value each other by putting a value on the other as well as putting a value on them-self. (Of course, God doesn't 'need' to be valued because He is all Value and He doesn't hate Himself.)

I felt that I was supposed to strive to get rid of my personality, strengths, and weaknesses. But that is not what the Lord wants. He created us the way we are, and He said it was very good. It is not about disregarding and discounting me but allowing who I 'truly' am to flourish. To let the Holy Spirit take all of who I am and go with me in partnership, as one. It is all about freedom to be real, not pretending. I was enthralled with the Lord but down on myself. Shamed. Freedom from this comes from being convinced of His love. Being rooted in His love. Being fully persuaded of His love.

I am free from the shame that had its tentacles in everything I would think or do. I had been listening to shame and let it leave me with a distorted view of God's work in me. Finding the True Love of God, that ugly voice of shame was unmasked. Now I am free to live fully as a child of the Lord's. I am free to be real, known for who I am.

- Reality over image
- Sincerity over pretentiousness
- Honesty over deceit

No more land of pretense.

To give up serving my reputation and finally trust in God's love. I do not need to defend myself to make sure others like me. When I know the Father loves me completely my reputation is secure in His hands, I will never again have to appeal for the approval of others.

When you know you're loved TOTALLY, you will never feel threatened again.

⇒ **Threatened means:**—to take hostile action against someone in retribution for something done or not done; intimidate, bully, blackmail or terrorize; endanger, cause to be vulnerable or at risk.

There is a tipping-point. When you lift your one foot, God is going to be your counter-balance, and He won't let you fall.

⇒ **Tipping-point means:**—the critical point in a situation, process or system beyond which a significant and often unstoppable effect or change takes place; crossing a certain threshold and gaining significant momentum, triggering an irreversible change.

Fully persuaded!

Where God affirms my worth in Him, His love for me, I won't need to seek its substitute from others or from 'things.' When I know I am **TOTALLY** loved, I will feel secure in His completely outstanding love. And where I know God overlooks my flaws I can overlook them in others.

Fifth

I am excited to end our study with this. From the Old Covenant of Law, we have a paradigm shift.

Read John 13:34-35 (bookmark):

Fill in all of the rest of **verse 34** below:
"A new command I give you...

_____

Also read John 15:12:

How are we to love each other?

_____

If there is a new command, what was the old command?

Please look up Matthew 22:34-40:

These verses are describing the greatest commandment in 'the what' in **verse 36** ? _____

Here we have Jesus summing up the Law.

Below please write out the greatest commandment in the Law from verse 37:

_____
_____

The first and greatest commandment. The second is like it. What is the second greatest commandment in the Law?

Write it out below from verse 39:

_____

What hangs on these two commands?

All the what in **verse 40**? _____ and the _____

The Old Covenant was to love God and to love your neighbor that about sums it up, **right**?

Go back to John 13:34:

Now we see again that Jesus gave a new command in a New Covenant through grace, not of Law. This is our reality. In fact, we struggle to live in this new reality. The reality is that this New Covenant begins with what He has done; not with what we do. **Seriously, this is new and different.**

Let this next sentence sit in your heart.

Love each other as Jesus has loved you!!

Interesting? Only after knowing this love, then and only then, will all men know that we are His disciple when we love one another **FROM** being loved. To the degree, we know and are aware of being loved, to this degree will we love. Here it is again.....Until you let yourself be loved by Him, you will not grasp how to love others.

In John 15:12 Jesus clearly says what? Please write it out:

_____

This is real, genuine and sincere it's not about acting or even about a command. It is an overflow. We don't have to mimic love or try to drum it up, or even see how Jesus loved and then copy Him. We are not actors and actresses starring in a lead role on how to show love.

God transforms our hearts by His heart of love for us.

Jesus loves you and demonstrated that love to you in John 15:13. What does this verse say that the greatest love looks like?

_____

Jesus did that!!

Jesus defined friendship. He laid down His life for His friends. He was others focused. **Our friendships with people stem from being rooted in THIS love.**

God's Covenant love!

We live **OUT** of the fullness of the depth of His love. Most Christians think of God's love in terms of following His heart and example through giving out His love as Jesus Christ would... But it's different than that... it is, in fact, being the host that the Holy Spirit moves through as a conduit directly downloading His True Love straight into the heart of another, physically imparting His Love!!

We have everything we need to live a godly life, to live for the glory of God, to live a life pleasing to Him. We have an eternal covenant, an unshakeable Kingdom and the best part of all the King of the Kingdom. We are complete and lack nothing!

Nothing can separate us from that love, and His love is big enough for everyone.

Once we understand this, then we can spend our time reminding each other of the tremendous blessing of the most incredible love imaginable and enjoy each other in that love. We can spend our time together praising the One who set us free and gave us life.

'How great is our God' is not a question it is a statement. Our God is Great! God holds a status all His own! He is our life! He is with us, for us, in us, present in everything and is everywhere with us at every moment loving us!

Galatians 2:20 says, **"I have been crucified with Christ and I no longer live, but Christ lives in me. The life I now live in the body, I live by faith in the Son of God, who loved me and gave himself for me."**

I started this study with this statement:

One of my burning desires is to have a passion for the Lord. He showed me that if I truly want this.........Then I must study hard Jesus' passion for me!! In other words, study hard Jesus' **LOVE** for me. I've just got to know that somebody **TOTALLY** loves me. And I know I am not alone.

As we have seen at the end of this study, if we want to love **others** with True Love, this particular kind of love comes as we study hard Jesus' love for us. From there will be the flow of love...

There is a powerful difference — a life revelation difference.

My hope is that after completing this study, you have your OWN story. That you have a clearer understanding of the details of God's perfect plan and I pray that a depth of love is forming down deep inside of you as you have realized the powerful reality of God's covenant love. That everything God does is based on covenant.

Is a new awareness emerging of what it means to be a friend of God? Ask the Lord to let this grow stronger and stronger bringing you confidence that cannot be taken away.

There is nothing I desire more than to have people know the **Love** that God has for them and to love Him back. This I believe is by far the most important thing that anyone can know in all of life. To fully grasp and be rooted and fully persuaded of this intense kind of True Love and as a result be whole, loved and content. Keep this constantly fresh in your heart going back to the basics… back to the covenant…….

He is amazing and… you are amazing.

He **TOTALLY** loves you!!!

Personal Guide

Thank you for your interest in investing your heart into this adventure. Sometimes it is nice to have a few details on useful techniques that may enhance how you can better glean from what an author is trying to speak from the narrative of their heart. I have included a Personal / Leader Guide on the last pages of this book. As you read through my thoughts on worship and prayer, they are coming from the angle of leading a group. But my hope is that you can also incorporate some aspects of this into your personal encounters with the Lord. Each of us is unique, so the reason I include this section is to share a bit of what has enriched my life over the years.

Blessings,

Debbie

Leader Guide

Dear Leader,

Thank you for your desire in leading this study called *Rooted in His Love.* From the bottom of my heart, I want to say thank you for your faithfulness and for putting your trust in this, as I know there is a sacrifice in leadership. I have had you in mind all throughout the writing of this study. As I visualized groups gathering together, I have pictured your heart. It could very well be that this is the first study you have led, or it could be that you are seasoned in facilitating a group. Either way, I have been in prayer for you. I wish that I could be there with you in person, right with you getting to know the different people that have come to glean and soak and take away a new wisdom and insight into the loving, caring and compassionate heart of God.

As a leader, it is so rewarding to watch other's grow and burst forth into what they were created to see and become. Giving your time and a listening ear and encouragement is truthfully what most people are craving when they come into your group, that they may feel noticed and heard. As you touch the heartache and the joy of those in your group I know that the Lord will indeed bless you.

This study was written for His glory, and I pray that He shows off that glory in your midst. His presence is the best!

Lovingly,

Debbie

-This guide offers suggestions for those who would be facilitating and leading a group for this seven-week study and can also be incorporated for personal reflection -

Rooted in His Love

by Debbie Jones

Worship:

Worship is not just a song but a lifestyle. Worship is a banquet in which God is the host. It is first and foremost an enjoyable and rich feasting on all that God is for us in Jesus. The more we worship Him, the more intimately we will know Him. The closer we come to know Him the more, it will be that we have Him as our focus and the more we will want to hear His voice. Worship is about having a relationship with God and is not necessarily easy to describe. It's more about the heart than the mind. To put it simply it is love expressed. Our greatest honor and privilege in life is to worship the Lord in the brightness of vivid sincerity.

Music is a powerful part and one of the key components for you personally or in facilitating a place for people to receive from the Lord and give Him honor. Playing worship recordings in the background as people mingle and chat keeps a heightened level of the beauty of the Lord flowing. As a leader, helping others to delight in God will change their perspective in the most unimaginable of ways. Worship recordings are available at bookstores or can be downloaded. You can print out the lyrics for the songs (noting the copyright laws) and hand them out so everyone can be in unison. If you have a large group or even a small relatively open and confidently transparent group, singing together can be a great blessing. Worship is a time of love. Alone or in a group God pours out His love on us, and we pour out our love to Him.

Prayer:

Intimacy is nurtured in communication, and prayer is a connection with the Lord that is vital. We assume most people are praying. The church believes its members are spending time every day in prayer. The truth is that the majority of people, including the most 'devout' are only spending microscopic amounts of time, about 15 seconds to maybe 5 to 10 minutes a day on average in prayer. Churches are so filled with programs that they hardly have time to pray. We bookend meetings with an opening prayer and sometimes a closing one just to make sure we have brought God into it.

In Jack Hayford's book *Prayer is Invading the Impossible*, there is a quote that states, "About two feet ahead and slightly to the left, son, there's an entry point into a better realm than ours. The problem is finding how to catch up with it!" To get to this dimension is to see things, not from our perspective but we get to peer into what is going on, on heaven's side of things. I have noticed that in some people's lives, including mine, there comes a time when our routine prayer becomes - not enough. The talk about prayer being time set aside as, "I meet with God while I am driving to work," or "I get my cup of coffee and my Bible and my prayer going first thing in the morning" just doesn't cut it for us anymore. We want more. What happens when we really really meet with God? These are times when we have life changing encounters with God. This not given to the faint hearted but to those with a relentless pursuit of God in the daily circumstances of life.

What is the true purpose of prayer? Isn't it constant continued fellowship with the most loving gracious all-knowing powerful holy God? Giving the Lord the fullest response of our heart, fixing our attention fully on His face. Prayer is an outpouring of our soul. Unreserved love on display. Could this be one of the highest forms of worship? When we pray, our focus turns to the Lord as we behold Him. Expressions of passionate adoration flow from the depths of our being and stem from an inward attitude of pure worship of God.

As a leader, you may be passionate about the importance of prayer. Leading your group to these encounters may be why you wanted to lead this study. However, we realize that prayer can be intimidating and we want to respect that people are growing at their own pace, and this even applies to you as the leader. Perhaps you feel you aren't cut out to lead an in-depth prayer time. That is OK. And besides it takes time for people to feel comfortable with each other and this is a part of the group that will unfold as the weeks go on.

Another key to a unified group is various forms of prayer. A sheet of paper can be passed around making it available for people to write down their prayer requests. One person from the group can type them up or scan them and send them out to those that would like to participate in an email prayer chain. Knowing what is going on in other people's lives can help us see their real issues instead of maybe the rose colored glasses that might lead us to believe that no one else has problems. God answers prayer, and this is exciting to witness and to share that back with the group.

Forming a group:

There are many ways to gather together a group of people. In your neighborhood or through or at your church. These locations can be the perfect extension for developing a way to get to know other people. The reason for the group can have the distinct intent of sharing the Gospel. Or, the unique purpose could be coming into the knowledge of the depth of the love of God so you can encourage those you wave to as you pull in and out of your driveway. What you will learn in this study is life revolutionizing! Many people attend church every week but have not come to the place of an actual encounter with God. In whatever way you come together, His love is circulating in the atmosphere when the topic of this book is the subject of discussion.

In the role of the leader, God has already equipped you with His strength as you rely on Him for guidance. The best group results in each member having opportunity to share what God has been revealing to them personally. The group will benefit by witnessing the Lord's touch on one another. Providing some structure and sensitivity will help promote this environment. Being mindful that there are outgoing talkers that may have a tendency to give every detail of their story and thus not allocating adequate time for the shyer or the bit reserved to speak into the gathering.

Some leaders wonder after the group starts the first week if they should continue to invite new people to join. The Lord has a divine appointment for each of us, and His invitation to come and be involved is always extended. He knows the perfect intersection for everyone, even if we aren't exactly sure what that looks like in any one person's life. If it works for your group, 'the more, the merrier,' within the limitations of space and the ability for 'all to shine', are good sayings to tuck into the pocket of our leadership influence.

Other ideas:

◆ Before the first study, prepare a sign in sheet for people to put down their names, addresses, phone numbers and email addresses. Bring pens.

◆ If your group is large, you may want to have nametags available so people can feel more comfortable getting acquainted. And sometimes people can't remember the name of someone they know they have met in the past, and this alleviates the awkwardness of having to ask.

♦ A basket or some other way to collect money if people will be paying right then for their copy of the book.

♦ You may want to have a potluck or refreshments at the first meeting; this is a good way of promoting fellowship.

♦ Spend some time the first week getting to know each other. You may want to have a few easy to answer questions prepared. Questions such as—what is your favorite room in your house and why? Or what is your favorite hobby? Something to break the ice and let people laugh and have fun.

♦ Set up the room the way you feel it works best for community, worship, prayer and study. It could be a circle or if a large group, tables with table leaders assigned to each table. It is harder to share once it gets past 10 or 12 people.

♦ You may want to go over a few confidentiality guidelines. What is shared in the group stays in the group. It is not a good idea to bring up negative bashing toward our spouse, family, and friends. Instead, have the sharing be uplifting and inspiring but real.

♦ Providing and raising questions to spark discussion will help each session flow more smoothly and will aid in the best use of effective time management. If possible allow about 90 minutes or more for worship, discussion, and prayer.

♦ It may be best to enlist an assistant or co-leader to help with contacting members, keeping the prayer chain thriving, giving feedback and being a substitute for you if you must be absent. Or you may want to rotate leaders, that may only work if each leader is willing to spend the necessary time to prepare for the meeting.

♦ As a leader, it is best to be a group member as well as a leader. Working through the material just as you would expect the other members of your group to do. It will be fresh in your heart and a current move of God in your life, staying in a right relationship with God so you can follow the leading of the Holy Spirit.

♦ Being sensitive, warm and caring realizing that as people work through this book, it will bring up personal emotions and feelings that they may or may not be comfortable in sharing. Don't worry about silence after you ask a question. People may need time to process and think. You may need to reword the question for a better response.

♦ Be prepared but be flexible. There may be times when it is evident that God is moving mightily in a particular way. Be able to transition from one thing to the next without the urgency to hurry and move on.

♦ Feel free to rearrange the order of this book to accommodate the needs of your group. There is added benefit to personalizing this with your story and journey as you illustrate.

♦ Pray for each member and each session. God is on the move, and He is revealing Himself!!

Thank you! Blessings on you and your group!

'Salvation Prayer'

Does a person need to pray a prayer to be saved?

The Bible says that salvation is of the heart. And it says in **Romans 10:13, "For whoever shall call upon the name of the Lord shall be saved."** This is a beckoning from the heart to rely upon and to put one's trust in God. A person prays because they are confirming what takes place in their heart. **Romans 10:9-10 says, "If you declare with your mouth, "Jesus is Lord," and believe in your heart that God raised him from the dead, you shall be saved. For it is with your heart that you believe and are justified, and it is with your mouth that you profess your faith and are saved."**

There is no 'formal' prayer of salvation mentioned in the Bible. Some people have adopted a specific style and put it in the form of a salvation prayer. But these prayers are usually variations of the above Scriptures. You can pray in your own words or repeat after someone as they are helping you, or recite the words that have been written down as a guide. But the key is your heart's true faith. But, please don't assume that this has taken place in your heart. Often we don't know when this 'officially' occurs because it's not necessarily about a rote prayer. If you are not certain, then come to the Lord Jesus Christ of Nazareth for forgiveness of your sin - past, present, and future. I have known people, however, who live in distress that they didn't say the prayer correctly and continue this over and over in repetition for years feeling uncertain and excluded. Some fear that in some way they can lose their salvation. The Lord's promises are true. Your prayer does not save you, your faith does. And, **"It is by grace you have been saved, through faith—and this is not from yourselves, it is the gift of God not by works, so that no one can boast." Ephesians 2:8-9**

The Gospel is Good News. Trust nothing and no one else, but Jesus! Put your trust in Jesus' perfect shed blood. **"It is finished." John 19:20.** He is the resurrection and the life. And He redeems you, and you become a new creation. A child with a Father that **TOTALLY** loves and adores you.

I believe that it is best to open up your heart to God in all honesty and sincerity. Even if you do not know the 'correct' thing to say He will lead you into true repentance….

Learn More About Grace Anthems and Join The Community By Subscribing

Go to:

GraceAnthems.com

Made in the USA
Middletown, DE
11 June 2017